Restaurant Graphics

First published in the United States of America by:
  Rockport Publishers, Inc.
  146 Granite Street
  Rockport, Massachusetts 01966-1299
  Telephone: (508) 546-9590
  Fax: (508) 546-7141

Distributed to the book trade and art trade
in the United States by:
  North Light, an imprint of
  F & W Publications
  1507 Dana Avenue
  Cincinnati, Ohio 45207
  Telephone: (800) 289-0963

Other Distribution by:
  Rockport Publishers
  Rockport, Massachusetts 01966-1299

ISBN 1-56496-255-5

10 9 8 7 6 5 4 3 2 1

Designer: Mimi Park and Albert Rufino
Cover Photograph: **RESTAURANT**
            Casa Havana

            CLIENT
            Columbia Sussex/
            Westin Casurian

            DESIGN FIRM
            Associates Design

            ART DIRECTOR
            Chuck Polonsky

            DESIGNER/ILLUSTRATOR
            Mary Greco

Additional photography by: Kevin Thomas Photography

Manufactured in China
by Regent Publishing Services Limited

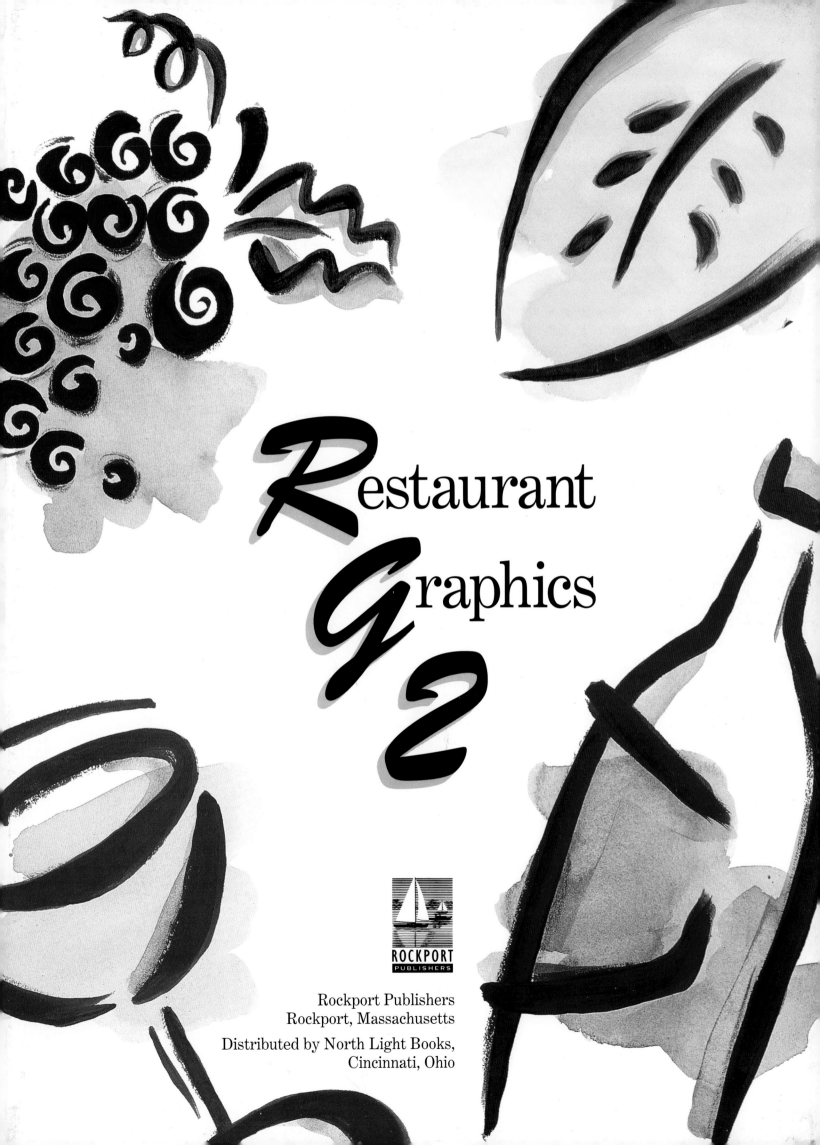

Restaurant Graphics 2

ROCKPORT
PUBLISHERS

Rockport Publishers
Rockport, Massachusetts

Distributed by North Light Books,
Cincinnati, Ohio

Contents

For Many Happy Returns:
Satisfy Their Visual Appetite

Marketing savvy and technology continue to expand graphic programs for restaurants. A generation ago, a neighborhood restaurant opened with little more than a sign and a plastic menu; these materials conveyed its neighborhood roots and feel. Today, restaurants of all sizes use restaurant professionals to develop marketing plans: accomplished chefs, noted restaurant architects and successful designers are called upon to help target groups of diners such as the ever-exploring public, diehard food lovers, and local critics. A good media review translates into increased popularity, expanding a restaurant's market beyond its neighborhood—hopefully into a "destination" restaurant for people throughout the area.

The role of graphics in restaurants and the impact of brand identity is expanding, as evidenced by the success of theme restaurants. Driven by innovative marketing, theme locations integrate brand image, broad food selection, entertainment, and shopping through the visual combination of strong architecture, graphics, video, and on-site retail merchandising. As a result, many diners expect visual reward as well as value when dining out. A client of ours with a midtown Manhattan location consistently had received praise for great value in its food, yet was criticized for its outdated look. The restaurant's new marketing strategy called for more than a cosmetic update of the location; it sought to reestablish presence in a competitive location by adopting a new brand identity with bolder colors, brighter interiors, and more visual signage. The new logo is the centerpiece for interior graphics, menus and related merchandise.

More and more, a logo has to have brand strength. Many metropolitan restauranteurs plan for success and expansion from the start. For these entrepreneurs, the initial question in logo development is whether the proposed logo will work as well in Phoenix as on the East and West Coasts. The expectation and demand is that the new logo succeeds for more than the traditional uses such as menus, stationery, and signage. It must also succeed on packaging, retail collateral and increasingly, on the Internet's World Wide Web.

Likewise, the function of a menu continues to change. Menus need to be modular to incorporate daily specials and promotions. Restauranteurs often want to change menus on a daily and weekly basis, so the designer needs to create menu templates that the eatery's staff can update. The challenge for restauranteurs and graphic designers is to create simple, well-organized menus with visual appeal. Good menu design enhances the pleasure of dining, increases customer spending, and encourages repeat business.

The Web home page, a new marketing tool, allows the restauranteur to reach customers. An interactive format will allow prospective customers to learn about seasonal menu changes and special events, order foods and read about other establishments operated by a particular restaurant group—all in a mouse click. Our design firm, PM Design, will continue to develop home pages with our restaurant clients, with its use as a marketing tool in mind.

Technology and smart marketing are critical to a restaurant's business operation, and they increase the likelihood of success. A strong restaurant graphics program helps create a compelling impression over a period of years. And yet, while the industry puts emphasis on target marketing and advance technology, trying to find new ways to reach the public, a restaurant's long-term success still hinges on value, service, and good food.   —PHILIP MARZO, PM DESIGN

An award-winning graphic design firm, PM Design has developed more than thirty restaurant programs in the last three years in the New York metropolitan area. With an emphasis in the restaurant and hospitality field, the firm's clients include food, wine, hotel and restaurant groups, and trade associations. The firm's design work has been featured regularly in national publications.

Bars & Grills

RESTAURANT
Harry's American Grill & Bar

DESIGN FIRM
Val Gene Associates

ART DIRECTOR/DESIGNER
Lacy Leverett

ILLUSTRATOR
Morrow Design, Shirley Morrow

RESTAURANT
Pepperoni Grill

DESIGN FIRM
Val Gene Associates

ART DIRECTOR
Lacy Leverett

PRINTING
Heritage Press

The design affords
the restaurant the ability
to print and laminate
menus as needed.

RESTAURANT
Mambo Grill

CLIENT
Restaurant Development Group

DESIGN FIRM
Marve Cooper Design

DESIGNERS
Marve Cooper, Grace Rapp

GRAPHICS
Craig Taylor-Yocat

PHOTOGRAPHER
Mark Ballogg

RESTAURANT/CLIENT
Gordon Biersch
Brewery Restaurant

DESIGN FIRM
Lance Anderson Design

ART DIRECTORS/DESIGNERS
Lance Anderson,
Richard Escasany

PHOTOGRAPHER
Craig Morey Studio

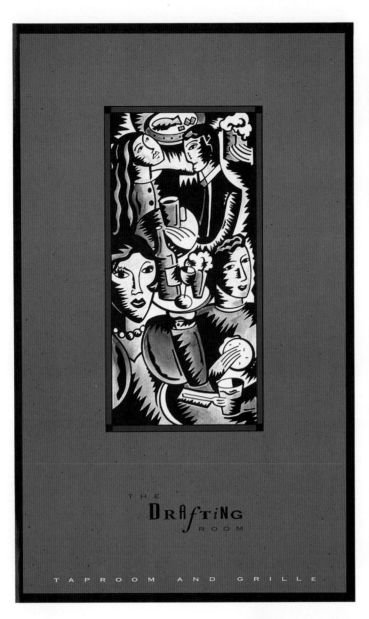

RESTAURANT
The Drafting Room

DESIGN FIRM
Associates Design

ART DIRECTOR
Chuck Polonsky

DESIGNERS/ILLUSTRATORS
Beth Finn, Shirley Bonk

Wholly hand-drawn,
this was done in pen
and ink with marker.

RESTAURANT
Nana Grill

CLIENT
Wyndham Anatole

DESIGN FIRM
Associates Design

ART DIRECTOR
Chuck Polonsky

DESIGNER/ILLUSTRATOR
Jill Arena

RESTAURANT
Waves

CLIENT
Marriott Hotels

DESIGN FIRM
Associates Design

ART DIRECTOR
Chuck Polonsky

DESIGNER
Beth Finn

ILLUSTRATOR
Kathy Bridgeman

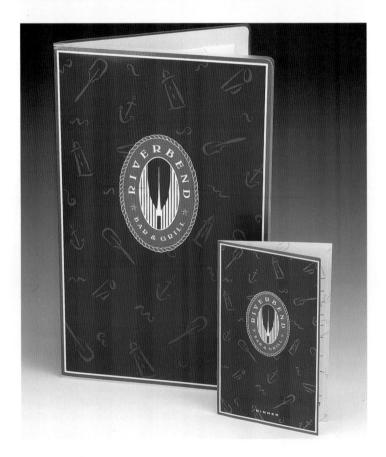

RESTAURANT
Riverbend Bar & Grill

CLIENT
Marriott Philadelphia Airport

DESIGN FIRM
Associates Design

ART DIRECTOR
Chuck Polonsky

DESIGNER/ILLUSTRATOR
Shirley Bonk

PAPER
Carolina Cover

RESTAURANT
Allie's American Grille

CLIENT
Marriott Hotels

DESIGN FIRM
Associates Design

ART DIRECTOR
Chuck Polonsky

DESIGNER
Bobbie Serafini

ILLUSTRATOR
Jill Arena

PAPER
Carolina Cover

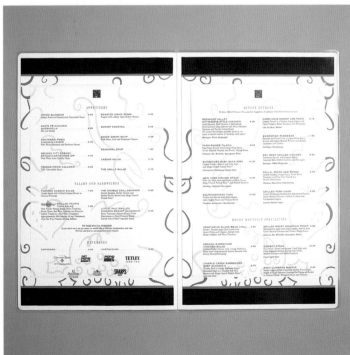

RESTAURANT
Kerry's Grill Room

DESIGN FIRM
Associates Design

ART DIRECTOR
Chuck Polansky

DESIGNER/ILLUSTRATOR
Mary Greco

RESTAURANT
Broad Ripple Brew Pub

CLIENT
John Hill,
Broad Ripple Brew Pub

DESIGN FIRM
Dean Johnson Design

ART DIRECTORS
John Hill, Scott Johnson

DESIGNER
Scott Johnson

ILLUSTRATORS
Scott Johnson, Lori Fox

This hand-drawn illustration
was scanned and converted
in Adobe Illustrator.

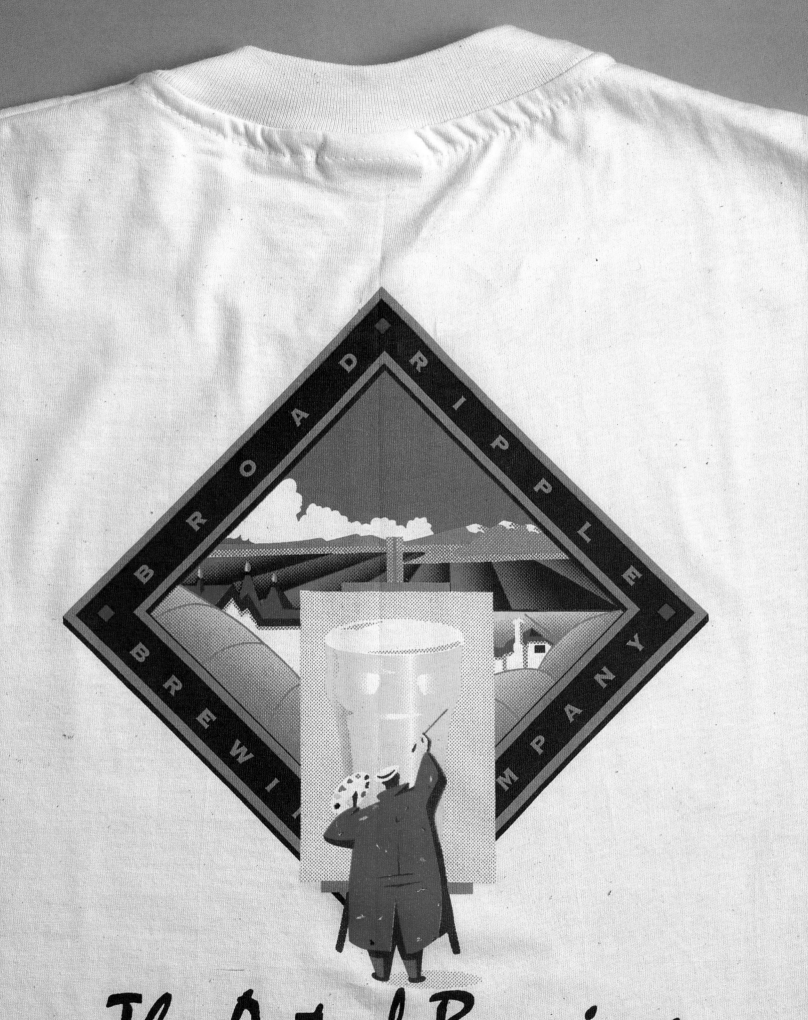

The Art of Brewing

RESTAURANT/CLIENT
Some Guys Pizza

DESIGN FIRM
Dean Johnson Design

ALL DESIGN
Mike Schwab, Bruce Dean

In the hand-drawn and photocopied art, the type is Mac-generated; the acrylic painting is based on the pop art of Roy Lichtenstein; for the collage, the works of Henri Matisse were used for inspiration.

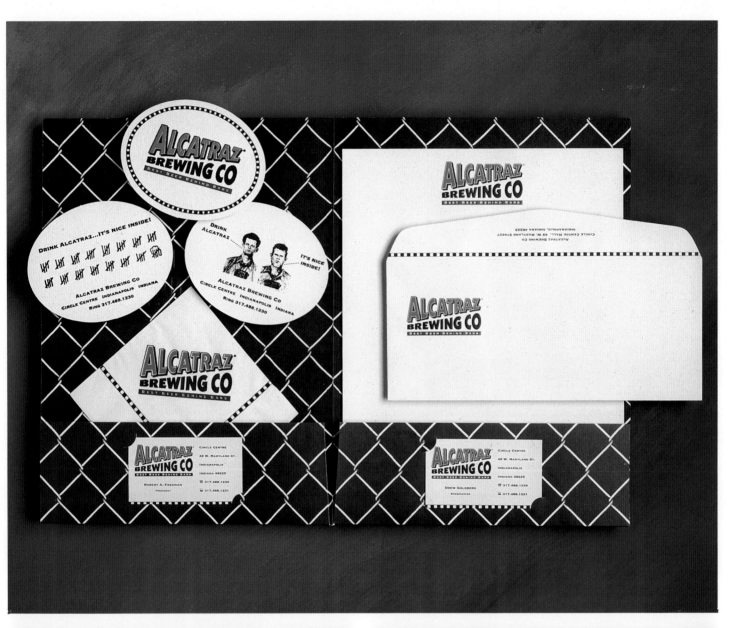

RESTAURANT
Alcatraz Brewing Co.

CLIENT
California Cafe
Restaurant Corp.

DESIGN FIRM
Lance Anderson Design

ALL DESIGN
Lance Anderson

PAPER/PRINTING
Nationwide Sandpiper

RESTAURANT
General Restaurant

CLIENT
Genesee Brewing Co.

DESIGN FIRM
McElveney & Palozzi Graphic
Design Group

ART DIRECTORS/DESIGNERS
Matthew Nowicki,
Stephen J. Palozzi

PHOTOGRAPHER
Buschner's Studio

RESTAURANT
Wasatch Front Tavern

CLIENT
Schirf Brewing Company

DESIGN FIRM
Harris & Love, Inc.

ART DIRECTOR
Kathy Lesh, Andy Cier

DESIGNER
Kathy Lesh

The beer logos were designed
in Macromedia FreeHand;
the flowing type in Adobe
Illustrator. Everything was
laid out in QuarkXPress.

RESTAURANT
Longhorn Saloon & Grill

DESIGN FIRM
Core Graphics

DESIGNER
Mike Park, Wes Wickham

The design for this piece
was done in Adobe Photoshop;
text and assembly in
Adobe PageMaker.

RESTAURANT
Rising Star Grill

CLIENT
Metromedia Restaurant Group

DESIGN FIRM
The Beaird Agency

ART DIRECTOR
David Howard

DESIGNER
Laura Trewin

Cedar fencepost used in hill
country of Texas, from where
the rising star concept comes.
When the "TTs" are stapled
on, an identifiable character
is provided—especially after
many have been attached
and torn off.

RESTAURANT/CLIENT
Washington Street Pub

DESIGN FIRM
Whitney-Edwards Design

ART DIRECTOR
Charlene Whitney-Edwards

DESIGNER
Barbi Christopher

ILLUSTRATOR
Charlene Whitney-Edwards

PAPER/PRINTING
Two colors on Becket Concept,
Glacier Mist

The illustrations were first
done in pencil, then scanned
into Adobe Photoshop;
the mastheads were done in
Adobe Illustrator. Everything
was compiled in QuarkXPress.

RESTAURANT/CLIENT
Paradise Bar & Grille

DESIGN FIRM
Enterprise Four

ART DIRECTOR
Phyllis Atkinson

DESIGNER/ILLUSTRATOR
Catherine Snyder-Kovacs

After creating an original painting of the logo, a transparency was made. Then it was scanned into Adobe Photoshop, where a file with PMS colors was created for those restaurants that couldn't print 4-color process. The menus were paintings. The cocktail napkins, all three glasses and coasters were done by scanning original line drawings in Macromedia FreeHand 5.0, with some blending. The mural was painted in acrylics; we also *faux'd* the walls.

RESTAURANT
Sea Dog Brewing Company

DESIGN FIRM
Adventure Advertising

ART DIRECTOR/DESIGNER
Joseph Ryan

ILLUSTRATOR
Jerry Sterman

PRINTING
Furbush Roberts,
American Coaster

RESTAURANT
Harry's Bar & Grill

CLIENT
Birdbrain Enterprise

DESIGN FIRM
The Menu Workshop

ART DIRECTOR
Liz Kearney

DESIGNERS
Liz Kearney, Wade Russell

ILLUSTRATOR
David Mellick

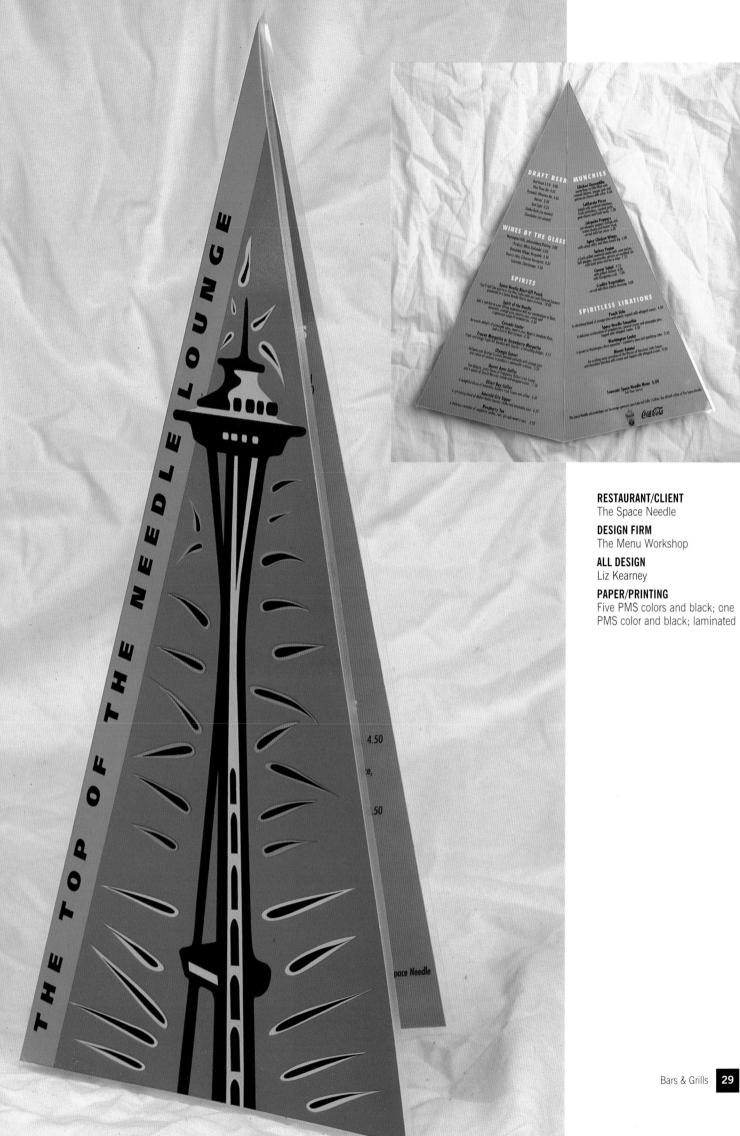

RESTAURANT/CLIENT
The Space Needle

DESIGN FIRM
The Menu Workshop

ALL DESIGN
Liz Kearney

PAPER/PRINTING
Five PMS colors and black; one
PMS color and black; laminated

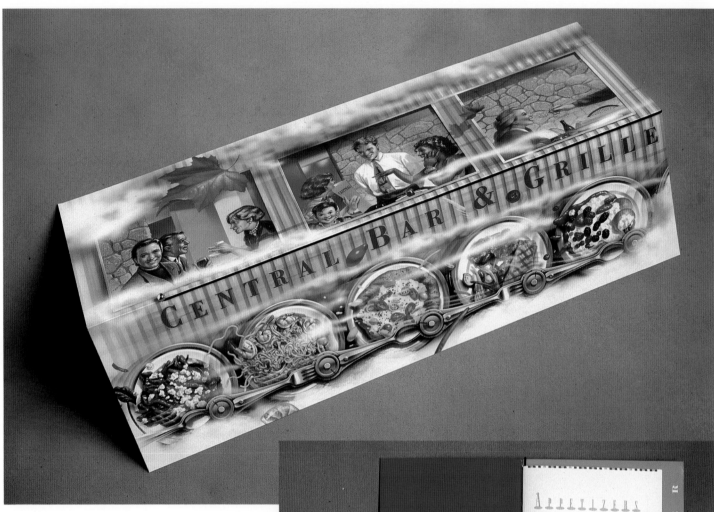

RESTAURANT
Central Bar & Grille

DESIGN FIRM
Shamlian Advertising

ART DIRECTOR
Fred Shamlian

DESIGNER
Stephen Bagi

ILLUSTRATOR
Justin Carroll

PRINTING
Graphicolor

The artwork was designed
to crop down for a one-third
page color advertisement.
The banner was done in Adobe
Illustrator and Dimensions,
with the type set in Illustrator
and Photoshop.

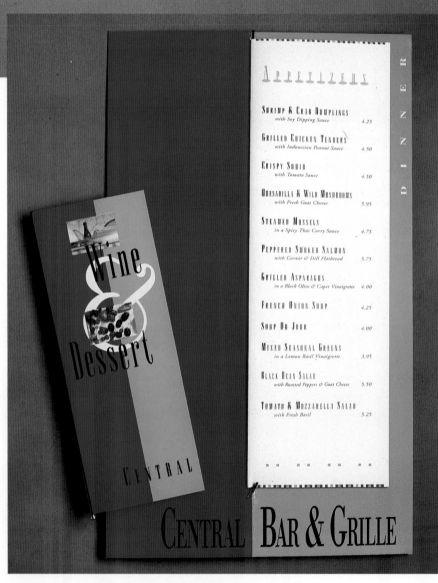

RESTAURANT
Spike's Jazz Bar

CLIENT
Hotel Principe Felipe

DESIGN FIRM
David Carter Design

ART DIRECTOR
Lori Wilson

DESIGNERS
Lori Wilson, Gary Lobue, Jr.

PAPER/PRINTING
Confetti; dull film lamination on front cover

Adobe Illustrator and Photoshop were utilized for the front cover artwork.

RESTAURANT
Soho Kitchen and Bar

CLIENT
Tony Golman

DESIGN FIRM
Sagmeister Inc.

ALL DESIGN
Stefan Sagmeister

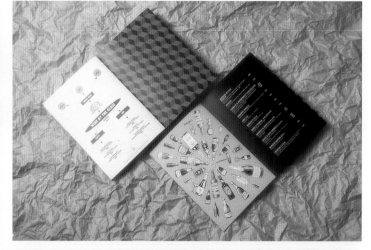

RESTAURANT
China Coast Pub

CLIENT
Regal Airport Hotel

ALL DESIGN
Timmy Kan

RESTAURANT/CLIENT
Angelic Brewing Company

DESIGN FIRM
Planet Design Company

ART DIRECTOR
Dana Lytle, Kevin Wade

DESIGNER
Dana Lytle

PAPER/PRINTING
Fox River Parchmarc
Bright White

Done in Macromedia FreeHand
and QuarkXPress, the menu
was designed to accommodate
future menu changes by
printing a second version,
sans copy.

RESTAURANT
Cigar Bar

CLIENT
Hudson Bar & Books, Ltd.

DESIGN FIRM
Tom Fowler, Inc.

ART DIRECTOR
Thomas G. Fowler

DESIGNERS/ILLUSTRATORS
Thomas G. Fowler,
Samuel Toh

Adobe Illustrator was used
to refine scanned artwork.

RESTAURANT
California Grill

CLIENT
Disney's Contemporary Resort

DESIGN FIRM
Disney Design Group

ART DIRECTORS
Jeff Morris, Renée Schneider

DESIGNER
Mark Frankel

PHOTOGRAPHER
Joe Brooks

PAPER/PRINTING
Champion Carnival White Vellum, 4-color process, die cut and embossed

A CAFE RESTAURANT & BAR

RESTAURANT
Farah's on the Avenue

CLIENT
Nick Farah

ALL DESIGN
Heather Heflin

Typesetting was done in
QuarkXPress; all illustrations
are acrylic and colored pencil.

APPETIZERS

BUFFALO WINGS .... 10 / 4.25 · 20 / 7.45
The stampede is on for Farah's tasty chicken wings served with bleu cheese dressing and
veggie sticks.

THAT ONION THING 4.95
A fresh whole onion blossom, sliced, hand-battered and fried. Served with Farah's dunking
sauce.

CHEESE STICKS 4.25
Farah's own homemade cheese sticks, fried and served hot with a tomato-ey marinara sauce.

'SHROOMS 3.95
A basketful of mushrooms, battered and fried golden, served with a dunking sauce--homemade
and worth waiting for.

CHICKEN FINGERS 5.25
Breaded chicken strips fried golden brown and served with BBQ sauce.

SPUDS 3.25
Potatoes cut the old-fashioned way and deep-fried to your liking.

FRIES 3.25
A large basket of crispy traditional shoestring french fries.

MEXICALI SPUDS 3.95
A south-of-the-border flavor of nacho cheese sauce, onions, and jalapeno peppers make these
'taters' a hot item!

SUPER NACHOS 5.95
A platter of nacho chips piled high with lettuce, tomatoes, onions, jalapenos, cheese sauce,
sour cream and your choice of chicken or beef. South-of-the-border salsa served on the side.

CHIPS AND SALSA 2.25
A large basket of fried tortilla chips served with farah's homemade salsa.

SALADS

DINNER SALAD 2.50
A fresh combination of iceberg lettuce, tomatoes, onions, green peppers, sprouts and carrots.

CHEF SALAD 5.50
A meal in itself, this salad is a mixture of the finest vegetables, cheese, eggs, turkey and ham.

GREEK SALAD 5.50
Farah's follows the traditional recipe of lettuce topped with Greek olives, pepperoncini, Feta cheese
and our house dressing.

SPINACH SALAD 4.95
A bed of spinach capped with sliced mushrooms, tomatoes, eggs, bacon, sprouts and house dressing.

CHARBROILED CHICKEN SALAD 5.75
Mixed greens topped with chunks of chicken, broccoli, tomatoes, onions, green peppers, cheese and
sprouts.

TABOULI SALAD 3.25
This healthy salad combines fresh parsley, diced tomatoes, onions, cucumbers, cracked wheat and
lemon juice.

SOUPS & QUICHE

Soup of the Day, New England
Clam Chowder, or French Onion

CUP 1.75
BOWL 2.95

SOUP & SALAD 3.75

QUICHE WITH SOUP OR SALAD 4.75
Farah's serves its homemade quiches with a
cup of the soup du jour or a tossed salad. Ask
your server for daily soup and salad special.

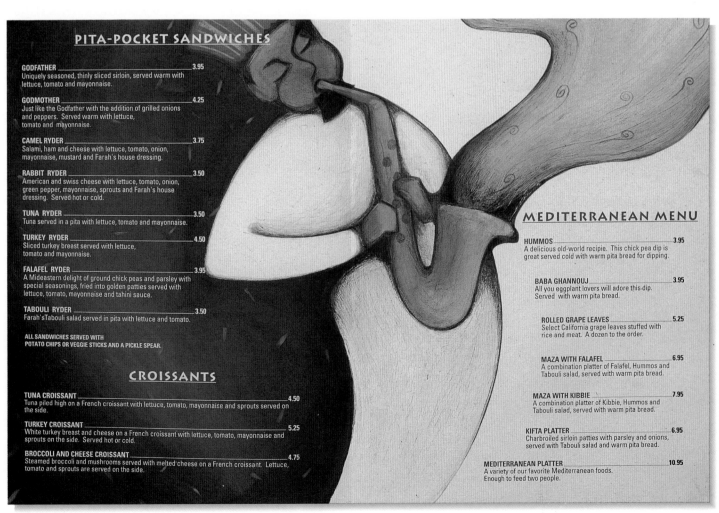

PITA-POCKET SANDWICHES

GODFATHER 3.95
Uniquely seasoned, thinly sliced sirloin, served warm with
lettuce, tomato and mayonnaise.

GODMOTHER 4.25
Just like the Godfather with the addition of grilled onions
and peppers. Served warm with lettuce,
tomato and mayonnaise.

CAMEL RYDER 3.75
Salami, ham and cheese with lettuce, tomato, onion,
mayonnaise, mustard and Farah's house dressing.

RABBIT RYDER 3.50
American and swiss cheese with lettuce, tomato, onion,
green pepper, mayonnaise, sprouts and Farah's house
dressing. Served hot or cold.

TUNA RYDER 3.50
Tuna served in a pita with lettuce, tomato and mayonnaise.

TURKEY RYDER 4.50
Sliced turkey breast served with lettuce,
tomato and mayonnaise.

FALAFEL RYDER 3.95
A Mideastern delight of ground chick peas and parsley with
special seasonings, fried into golden patties served with
lettuce, tomato, mayonnaise and tahini sauce.

TABOULI RYDER 3.50
Farah'sTabouli salad served in pita with lettuce and tomato.

**ALL SANDWICHES SERVED WITH
POTATO CHIPS OR VEGGIE STICKS AND A PICKLE SPEAR.**

CROISSANTS

TUNA CROISSANT 4.50
Tuna piled high on a French croissant with lettuce, tomato, mayonnaise and sprouts served on
the side.

TURKEY CROISSANT 5.25
White turkey breast and cheese on a French croissant with lettuce, tomato, mayonnaise and
sprouts on the side. Served hot or cold.

BROCCOLI AND CHEESE CROISSANT 4.75
Steamed broccoli and mushrooms served with melted cheese on a French croissant. Lettuce,
tomato and sprouts are served on the side.

MEDITERRANEAN MENU

HUMMOS 3.95
A delicious old-world recipie. This chick pea dip is
great served cold with warm pita bread for dipping.

BABA GHANNOUJ 3.95
All you eggplant lovers will adore this dip.
Served with warm pita bread.

ROLLED GRAPE LEAVES 5.25
Select California grape leaves stuffed with
rice and meat. A dozen to the order.

MAZA WITH FALAFEL 6.95
A combination platter of Falafel, Hummos and
Tabouli salad, served with warm pita bread.

MAZA WITH KIBBIE 7.95
A combination platter of Kibbie, Hummos and
Tabouli salad, served with warm pita bread.

KIFTA PLATTER 6.95
Charbroiled sirloin patties with parsley and onions,
served with Tabouli salad and warm pita bread.

MEDITERRANEAN PLATTER 10.95
A variety of our favorite Mediterranean foods.
Enough to feed two people.

Coffee
Shops

Dessert
Bars

Cafés

RESTAURANT/CLIENT
Beach Cafe

DESIGN FIRM
The Menu Workshop

ART DIRECTOR
Liz Kearney

DESIGNER/ILLUSTRATOR
John Rice

PHOTOGRAPHER
Charles A. Blackburn

RESTAURANT
California Lounge

CLIENT
School assignment

DESIGN FIRM
i.d. zign co.

DESIGNER
Danielle Hare

PHOTOGRAPHER
Joseph Hope

PRINTING
Kate's Paperie

This project was created
using Adobe Illustrator
and Photoshop.

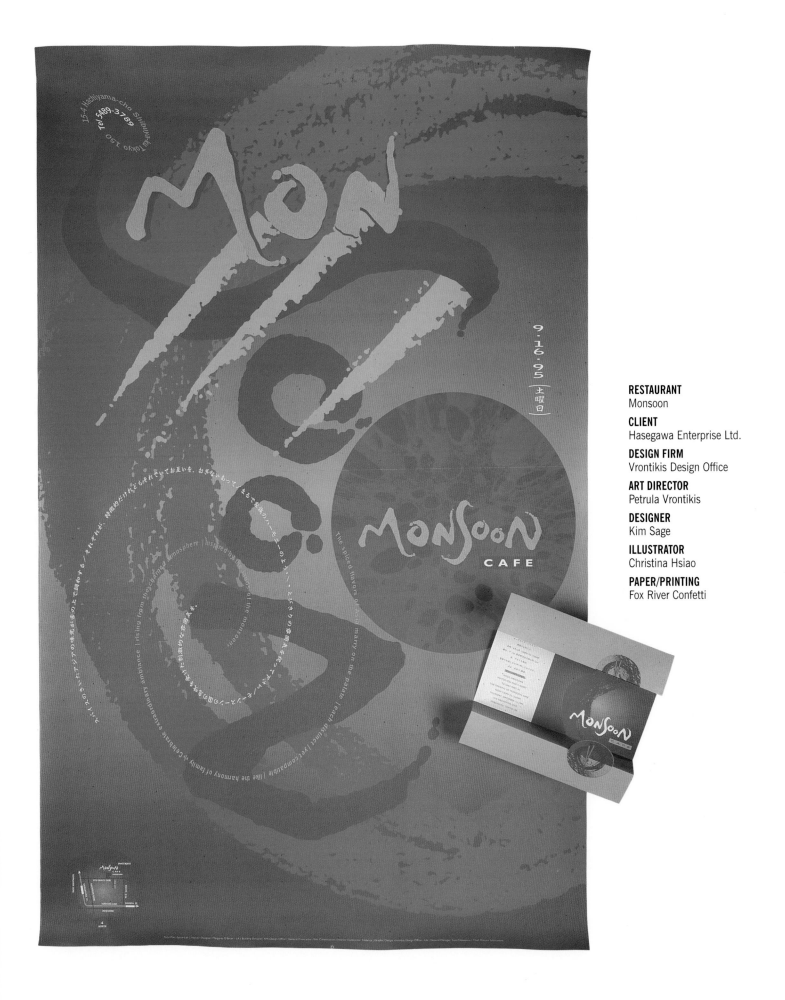

RESTAURANT
Monsoon

CLIENT
Hasegawa Enterprise Ltd.

DESIGN FIRM
Vrontikis Design Office

ART DIRECTOR
Petrula Vrontikis

DESIGNER
Kim Sage

ILLUSTRATOR
Christina Hsiao

PAPER/PRINTING
Fox River Confetti

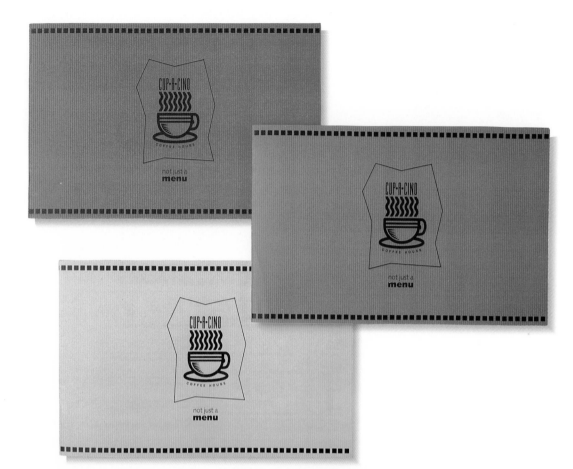

RESTAURANT
Cup•A•Cino Coffee House

CLIENT
Jennifer Bell

DESIGNER
Gloria Paul

ILLUSTRATORS
Various

PAPER/PRINTING
Wausau Astrobrights
60 lb. text/offset

This project was produced
on a Power Macintosh, using
Macromedia FreeHand.

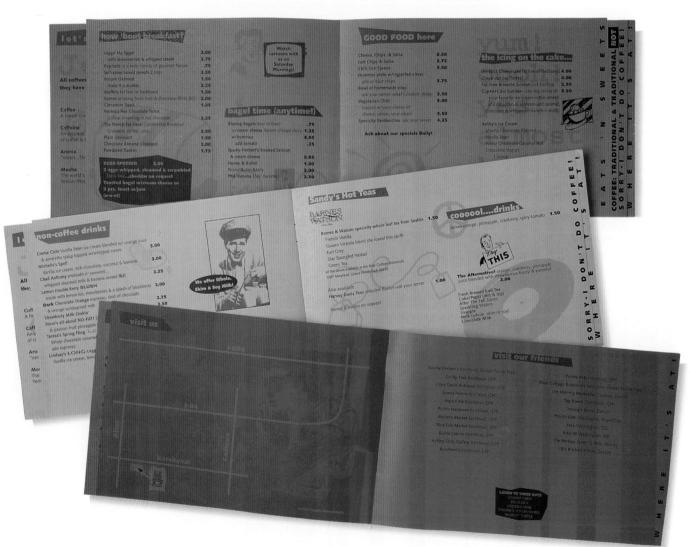

RESTAURANT
Crimson Moon Coffeehouse

CLIENT
Kara Williamson

DESIGN FIRM
Laura Jacoby

ALL DESIGN
Laura Jacoby

PAPER
Fox River Confetti
and Early American

The type and logo were hand-illustrated, then scanned and put together in QuarkXPress.

RESTAURANT
Arts Theatre Café

CLIENT
Phil Owens, Jo Phillips

DESIGN FIRM
Betty Soldi

ALL DESIGN
Betty Soldi

The calligraphy and illustrations were done with a dip ink pen; all typesetting was done in Macromedia FreeHand.

RESTAURANT/CLIENT
Timbuktuu Coffee Bar

DESIGN FIRM
Sayles Graphic Design

ALL DESIGN
John Sayles

PHOTOGRAPHER
Bill Nellans

Warm earth tones for ink
and paper colors were chosen
to reflect interior design
of the coffee house; the type
was hand-rendered.

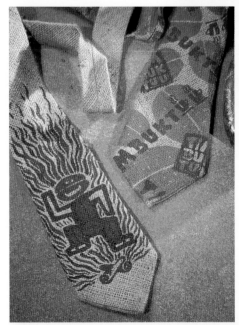

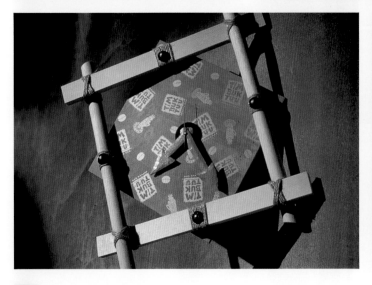

COFFEE CARES

BARISTAS, BAKERIES & BISTROS SUPPORTING PEOPLE WITH AIDS

RESTAURANT
Coffee Cares

CLIENT
Our House of Portland

DESIGN FIRM
Jeff Fisher Design

ALL DESIGN
Jeff Fisher

This image was created in Macromedia FreeHand.

RESTAURANT
Cafes Canal Place

CLIENT
Canal Place

DESIGN FIRM
Hornall Anderson Design Works, Inc.

ART DIRECTOR/DESIGNER
Jack Anderson

CALLIGRAPHER
Bruce Hale

RESTAURANT/CLIENT
Grounds Coffee World

DESIGN FIRM
Jeff Fisher Design

ALL DESIGN
Jeff Fisher

This project was created in Macromedia FreeHand, with Ray Dream addDepth used for three-dimensional effect.

RESTAURANT
Last Drop Coffee House

CLIENT
David Sokolow, Philip Cohen

DESIGN FIRM
Shelley Danysh Studio

ALL DESIGN
Shelley Danysh

This entire logo was hand-rendered.

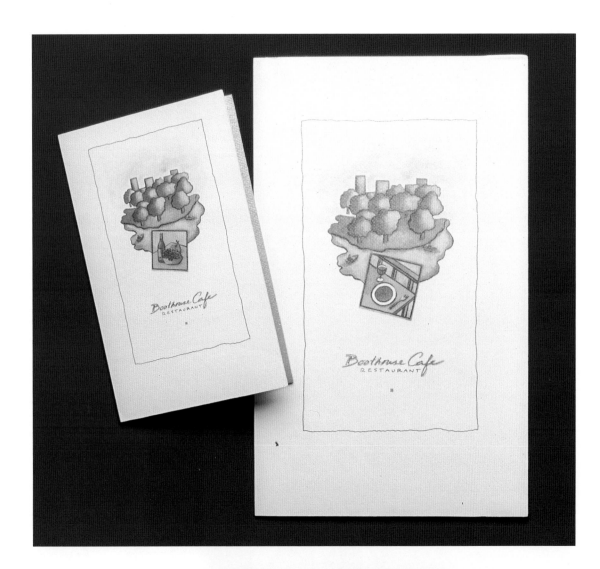

RESTAURANT
The Boathouse in Central Park

CLIENT
Tam Restaurant Group

DESIGN FIRM
PM Design

ART DIRECTOR/DESIGNER
Philip Marzo

ILLUSTRATORS
Lonnie Sue Johnson,
Philip Marzo

PHOTOGRAPHER
Geoff Reed

RESTAURANT
World Cafe

CLIENT
David Tech

DESIGN FIRM
Rusty Kay & Associates

ART DIRECTOR
Rusty Kay

DESIGNER
Susan Rogers

PHOTOGRAPHER
Bill VanScoy

RESTAURANT
Candle Cafe

DESIGN FIRM
Louise Fili Ltd.

ART DIRECTOR/DESIGNER
Louise Fili

PAPER/PRINTING
All recycled stock

Each component uses a
different image from
a vintage seed catalog.

RESTAURANT
The Café

CLIENT
Westin Hotel O'Hare

DESIGN FIRM
Associates Design

ART DIRECTOR
Chuck Polonsky

DESIGNER/ILLUSTRATOR
Shirley Bonk

RESTAURANT
Bonfamille's Cafe

CLIENT
Disney's Port Orleans Resort

DESIGN FIRM
Disney Design Group

ART DIRECTORS
Jeff Morris, Renée Schneider

DESIGNER
Mimi Palladino

ILLUSTRATOR
Michael Mohjer

WRITER
Tony Fernandez

PAPER/PRINTING
Warren Lustro Gloss;
cover: 3-color plus metallic
and overall dull varnish;
interior: 2-color plus metallic,
custom matched cream and
overall dull varnish

RESTAURANT/CLIENT
South Union Bakery
and Bread Cafe

DESIGN FIRM
Sayles Graphic Design

ALL DESIGN
John Sayles

RESTAURANT
Pulp—A Juice Bar

CLIENT
David Sokolow, Philip Cohen

DESIGN FIRM
Shelley Danysh Studio

ALL DESIGN
Shelley Danysh

This project was created with
Adobe Illustrator.

RESTAURANT
Juice Works

CLIENT
Bobby McGee's of Arizona

DESIGN FIRM
Associates Design

ART DIRECTOR
Chuck Polonsky

DESIGNER/ILLUSTRATOR
Beth Finn

RESTAURANT
Wienerwald Restaurants

CLIENT
Wienerwald 2000 GmbH

DESIGN FIRM
Factory Werbeagentur

ART DIRECTOR/DESIGNER
Dieter Heise

This image was created using Macromedia FreeHand and Adobe Photoshop.

RESTAURANT/CLIENT
Tippin's

DESIGN FIRM
Mallen and Friends

ART DIRECTOR/DESIGNER
Gary Mallen

PHOTOGRAPHERS
Wans Studio,
Ernie Block Studio

PRINTING
B & C Printing

ALL SEASONS CAFE

RESTAURANT
Cafe Maddalena

CLIENT
Maddalena Serra

DESIGN FIRM
Lance Anderson Design

ART DIRECTOR/DESIGNER
Lance Anderson

PRINTING
Walker Litho

CAFE MADDALENA

CHEF / PROPRIETOR
MADDALENA SERRA

MANAGER / PROPRIETOR
LANCE ANDERSON

TEL 916 235 2725
FAX 916 235 0639

AUTHENTIC ITALIAN AND
MEDITERRANEAN COUNTRY COOKING

CATERING AND TAKE-OUT AVAILABLE

5801 SACRAMENTO AVENUE
(ACROSS FROM THE OLD TRAIN STATION)
DUNSMUIR, CALIFORNIA 96025

RESTAURANT
All Seasons Cafe

CLIENT
Hyatt Hotels Corp.

DESIGN FIRM
Associates Design

ART DIRECTOR
Chuck Polonsky

DESIGNER
Jill Arena

PHOTOGRAPHER
Dave Slavinski

COMPUTER ARTIST
John Arena

Family Restaurants

RESTAURANT
Tony's Town Square Restaurant

CLIENT
Magic Kingdom,
Walt Disney World

DESIGN FIRM
Disney Design Group

ART DIRECTORS
Jeff Morris, Renée Schneider

DESIGNER
Mimi Palladino

ILLUSTRATORS
Don Williams, Peter Emslie,
Michael Mohjer, H.R. Russell,
Jim Story

WRITERS
Greg Ehrbar, Jim Story

PAPER/PRINTING
French Durotone, French
Parchtone (cover silk-screen,
deboss, 4-color process),
Deboss 4-color process,
Warren Lustro Gloss,
4-color process with die cuts

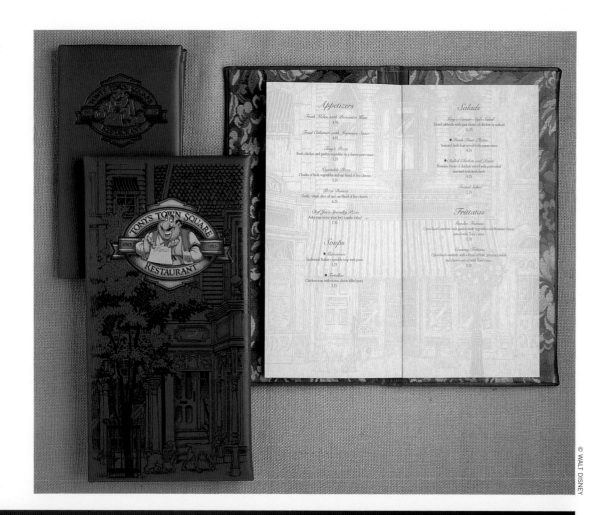

© WALT DISNEY

© WALT DISNEY

RESTAURANT
Crockett's Tavern

CLIENT
Disney's Fort Wilderness Resort

DESIGN FIRM
Disney Design Group

ART DIRECTORS
Jeff Morris, Renée Schneider

DESIGNERS
Thomas Scott,
Michael Mohjer

ILLUSTRATOR
Michael Mohjer

PAPER/PRINTING
Crosspoint Genesis, one color;
Menu board on Birchwood,
2-color screen print; Inserts are
French Butcher, two-color

RESTAURANT
Whispering Canyon Cafe

CLIENT
Disney's Wilderness Lodge

DESIGN FIRM
Disney Design Group

ART DIRECTOR
Jeff Morris, Renée Schneider

DESIGNER
Mimi Palladino

ILLUSTRATOR
Michael Mohjer

WRITER
Tony Fernandez

PAPER/PRINTING
French Speckletone, 3-color

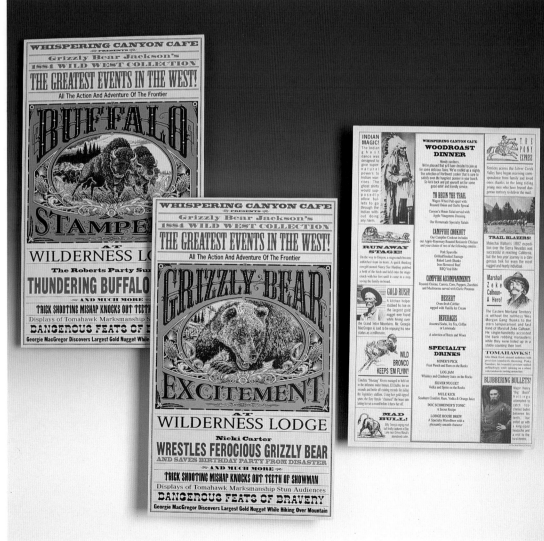

© WALT DISNEY

RESTAURANT
Boatwright's Dining Hall

CLIENT
Disney's Dixie Landings Resort

DESIGN FIRM
Disney Design Group

ART DIRECTORS
Jeff Morris, Renée Schneider

DESIGNERS
Mike Wood, Bob Holden,
Mimi Palladino

ILLUSTRATOR
Peter Emslie, Michael Mohjer

WRITER
Denise Bates Kathedar

PHOTOGRAPHER
Greg Ehrbar

PAPER/PRINTING
Menu: one color with die cut;
ruler: 2-color with die cut and
dull laminate; seating card:
James River Graphika, one
color; adult menu: James River
Graphika, 4-color process plus
one flat color; wine/drink menu:
Warren Lustro Gloss, 4-color
process, two flat colors, die cut
and matte laminate

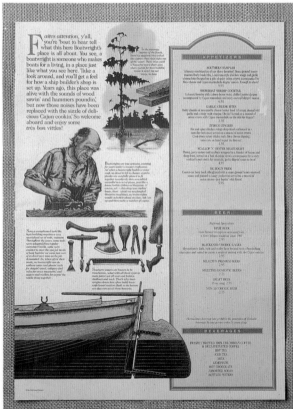

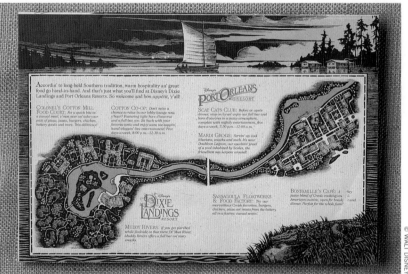

© WALT DISNEY

RESTAURANT
Liberty Tree Tavern

CLIENT
Magic Kingdom Park

DESIGN FIRM
Disney Design Group

ART DIRECTORS
Jeff Morris, Renée Schneider

DESIGNERS
Renée Schneider, Mark Frankel

ILLUSTRATORS
H.R. Russell, Peter Emslie,
Michael Mohjer

WRITER
Walt Disney Imagineering,
Tony Fernandez

PAPER/PRINTING
Adult menu: insert: Warren
Lustro Dull Cream, 4-color
process; cover: four different
vinyls, 4-color process silk-
screen, sculptured emboss, foil
stamp, two colors; children's
menu: Sundance Felt Adobe
Tan, one color, perforated; guest
check presenter: two colors of
vinyl, two colors of foil stamp

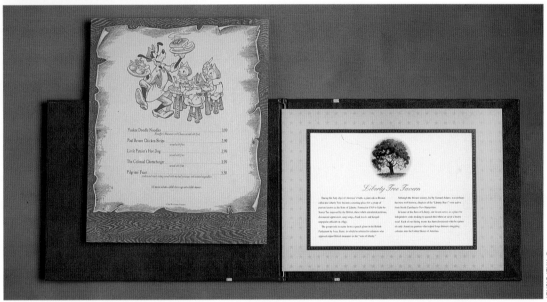

© WALT DISNEY

RESTAURANT
Olivia's Cafe

CLIENT
Disney Vacation Club

DESIGN FIRM
Disney Design Group

ART DIRECTORS
Jeff Morris, Renée Schneider

DESIGNERS
Thomas Scott, Robert Haines

ILLUSTRATORS
Dave Herrick, Joyce Stiglich

PHOTOGRAPHERS
John Petrey, Joe Brooks

CALLIGRAPHY
Rita Tyrrell

PAPER/PRINTING
Fox River Circa Select, 4-color
process; Simpson Starwhite
Vicksburg, 3-color with die cut

© WALT DISNEY

© WALT DISNEY

RESTAURANT
'Ohana

CLIENT
Disney's Polynesian Resort

DESIGN FIRM
Disney Design Group

ART DIRECTORS
Jeff Morris, Renée Schneider

DESIGNER
Michelle Nelson

ILLUSTRATOR
Don Williams

WRITER
Vernon Whitaker

PAPER/PRINTING
Federal Envirocote, 4-color process plus aqueous coating on front, one color on back

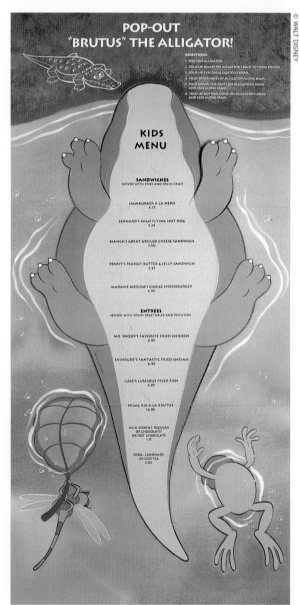

POP-OUT "BRUTUS" THE ALLIGATOR!

DIRECTIONS:
1. POP-OUT ALLIGATOR.
2. FOLD-UP BUMPS ON ALLIGATOR'S BACK TO FORM POINTS.
3. FOLD-UP EYES ON ALLIGATOR'S HEAD.
4. FOLD-DOWN SIDES OF ALLIGATOR ALONG SEAM.
5. FOLD-DOWN TOP JOINT ON ALLIGATOR'S ARMS AND LEGS ALONG SEAM.
6. FOLD-UP BOTTOM JOINT ON ALLIGATOR'S ARMS AND LEGS ALONG SEAM.

KIDS MENU

SANDWICHES
SERVED WITH FRIES AND FRESH FRUIT

HAMBURGER A LA NERO
4.75

BERNARD'S HIGH FLYING HOT DOG
3.25

BIANCA'S GREAT GRILLED CHEESE SANDWICH
3.50

PENNY'S PEANUT BUTTER & JELLY SANDWICH
3.25

MADAME MEDUSA'S CHOICE CHEESEBURGER
4.95

ENTREES
SERVED WITH FRESH VEGETABLES AND POTATOES

MR. SNOOP'S FAVORITE FRIED CHICKEN
4.95

EVINRUDE'S FANTASTIC FRIED SHRIMP
6.95

LUKE'S LUSCIOUS FRIED FISH
4.95

PRIME RIB A LA BRUTUS
14.95

MILK (LOWFAT, REGULAR OR CHOCOLATE) OR HOT CHOCOLATE
1.75

SODA, LEMONADE OR ICED TEA
2.00

RESTAURANT
Narcoosee's

CLIENT
Disney's Grand Floridian Beach Resort

DESIGN FIRM
Disney Design Group

ART DIRECTORS
Jeff Morris, Renée Schneider

DESIGNER
Mimi Palladino

ILLUSTRATOR
Peter Emslie

PAPER/PRINTING
Quintessence Remarque, 4-color process and die cut

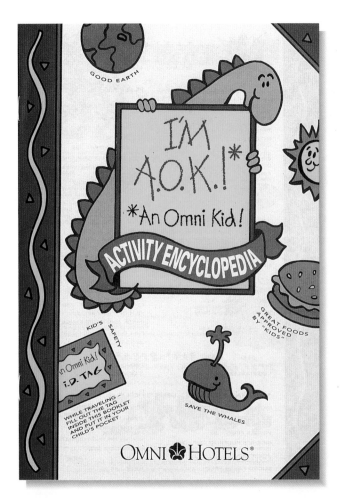

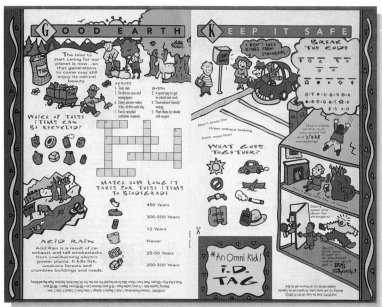

CLIENT
Omni Hotels

DESIGN FIRM
Associates Design

ART DIRECTOR
Chuck Polonsky

DESIGNER/ILLUSTRATOR
Shirley Bonk

CLIENT
Walker Bros. Pancake House

DESIGN FIRM
Associates Design

ART DIRECTOR
Chuck Polonsky

DESIGNER
Mary Greco

ILLUSTRATOR
Jill Arena

PHOTOGRAPHER
Larry Devera

RESTAURANT/CLIENT
Silo's Steakhouse

DESIGN FIRM
Scott Wright Design

ART DIRECTOR/DESIGNER
Scott Wright

PAPER/PRINTING
2-color on Genesis Milkweed

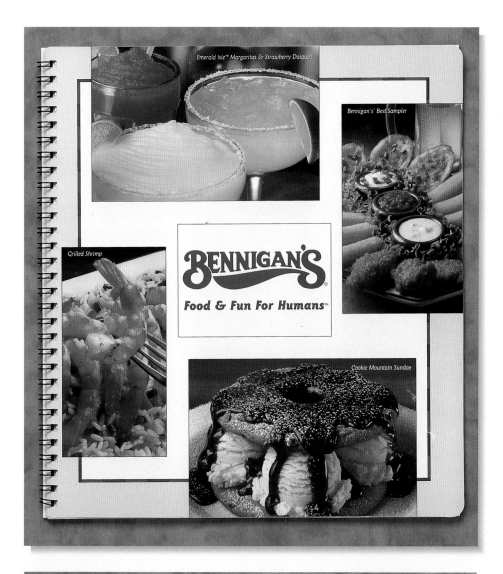

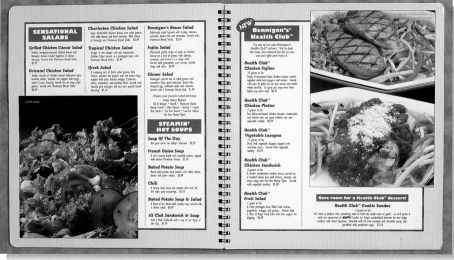

RESTAURANT
Bennigan's

CLIENT
Metromedia Restaurant Group

DESIGN FIRM
The Beaird Agency

ART DIRECTOR
David Howard

DESIGNERS
Scott Florence, David Howard

PHOTOGRAPHER
Rusty Hill

RESTAURANT
Bennigan's

CLIENT
Metromedia Restaurant Group

DESIGN FIRM
The Beaird Agency

ART DIRECTOR
David Howard

DESIGNERS
Scott Florence, Laura Trewin, David Howard

ILLUSTRATORS
Scott Florence, David Howard

PHOTOGRAPHER
Rusty Hill

Menu insert contains pop-up with sound chip that plays sounds of a bus running and honking each time menu insert is opened.

RESTAURANT
Montana Steak Company

CLIENT
Metromedia Restaurant Group

DESIGN FIRM
The Beaird Agency

ART DIRECTOR
David Howard

DESIGNER
Crethann Hickman

ILLUSTRATOR
David Howard

PAPER
Kimdura Buckskin

RESTAURANT/CLIENT
Mitzel's American Kitchen

DESIGN FIRM
The Menu Workshop

ART DIRECTOR
Liz Kearney

DESIGNERS
Liz Kearney, Wade Russel

ILLUSTRATOR
Shawn Hair

PAPER/PRINTING
4-color process
and two PMS colors

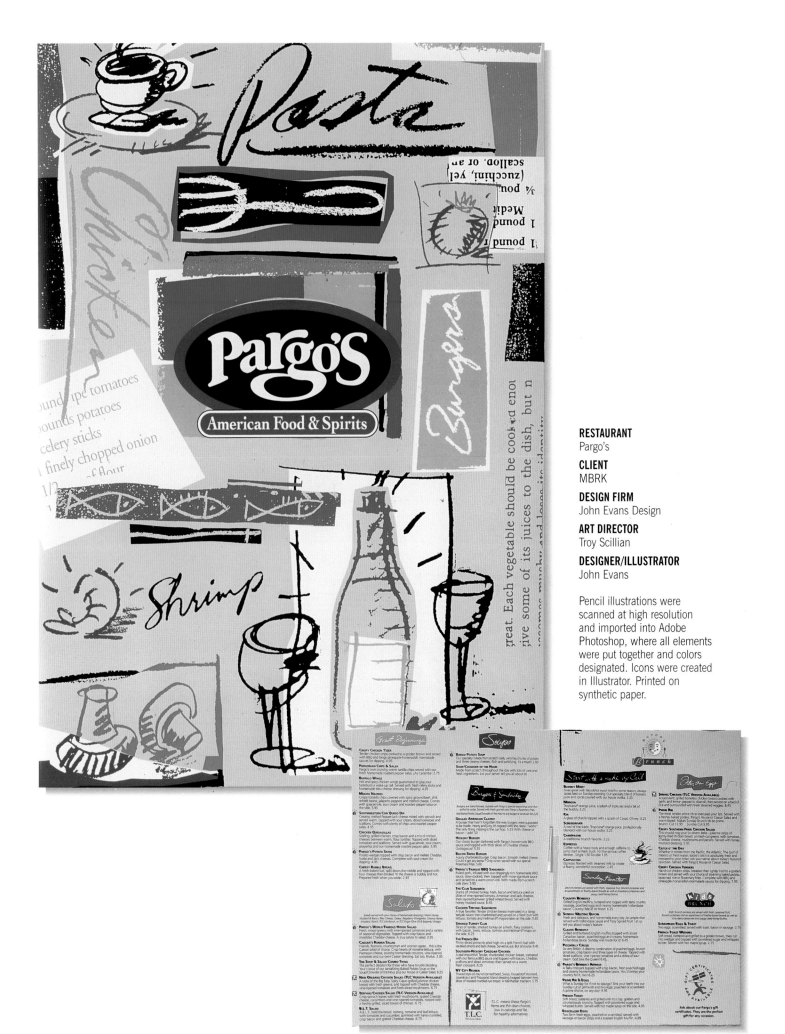

RESTAURANT
Pargo's

CLIENT
MBRK

DESIGN FIRM
John Evans Design

ART DIRECTOR
Troy Scillian

DESIGNER/ILLUSTRATOR
John Evans

Pencil illustrations were scanned at high resolution and imported into Adobe Photoshop, where all elements were put together and colors designated. Icons were created in Illustrator. Printed on synthetic paper.

Take Home or Eat Here

RESTAURANT/CLIENT
Ozzie G's

DESIGN FIRM
Bright & Associates

ART DIRECTORS
Keith Bright, Konrad Bright

DESIGNER/ILLUSTRATOR
Konrad Bright

RESTAURANT/CLIENT
Roadbird Broasted Chicken

DESIGN FIRM
GAF Advertising/Design

ALL DESIGN
Gregg A. Floyd

The chicken was produced by hand; the type was modified using Macromedia FreeHand.

DIVE! KIDS MENU

FRIED CHICKEN SUB
Crisp fried breast of chicken served on soft torpedo bun with pickles, lettuce and tomato on the side. 5.95

TURKEY BREAST TORPEDO
Oven roasted turkey breast served on soft torpedo bun with lettuce and tomato on the side. 5.95

TOASTED CHEESE TORPEDO
Soft torpedo bun with melted cheddar cheese. 4.95

SUB-DOG
Steamed all beef hot dog served on a soft torpedo bun. 4.95

HAMBURGER
Extra lean beef ground fresh in our galley daily. served on a soft baguette with lettuce and tomato on the side. 5.50
Cheeseburger 5.95

DIVE! FRIES
Top it off with choice of ketchup, cheese or barbecue sauce. 2.95

All sandwiches are served with fries.

DESSERTS

ICE CREAM
Chocolate, Vanilla or Strawberry 3.95

S'MORES
Graham crackers, milk chocolate and toasted marshmallows streaked with chocolate sauce. 4.95

CHOCOLATE CHUNK COOKIE
Baked fresh daily. 2.50

WARM COOKIE SUNDAE
Warm chocolate chunk cookie with white chocolate ice cream, hot fudge, whipped cream and trimmings. 4.95

DRINKS
Soft drinks and lemonade with free refills. 1.75

FOR KIDS 10 & UNDER

RESTAURANT
DIVE! Los Angeles and DIVE! Las Vegas

CLIENT
The Levy Restaurants/ Steven Spielberg and Jeffrey Katzenberger

DESIGN FIRMS
Adrienne Weiss Corporation, The Levy Restaurants

Seafood Restaurants

Tropical Fare

RESTAURANT
Skipjack's

CLIENT
Restaurant Concepts Inc.

DESIGN FIRM
PandaMonium Designs

ALL DESIGN
Raymond Yu

PAPER/PRINTING
Large-format inkjet; two spot colors and duotone on Simpson Evergreen Birch

The menu was designed in QuarkXPress. Table tents were designed in Macromedia FreeHand and QuarkXPress.

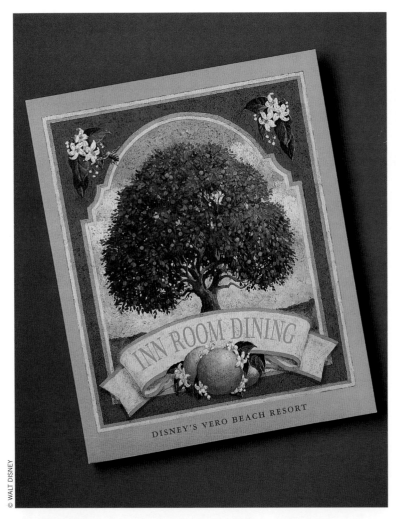

CLIENT
Disney's Vero Beach Resort

DESIGN FIRM
Disney Design Group

ART DIRECTORS
Jeff Morris, Renée Schneider

DESIGNER
Mimi Palladino

ILLUSTRATOR
H.R. Russell

PAPER/PRINTING
Champion Carnival Linen,
4-color process

RESTAURANT
Grand Floridian Cafe

CLIENT
Disney's Grand Floridian
Beach Resort

DESIGN FIRM
Disney Design Group

ART DIRECTORS
Jeff Morris, Renée Schneider

DESIGNER
Mark Frankel

ILLUSTRATOR
Jesse Clay

PAPER/PRINTING
Cover: Warren Lustro Dull,
4-color process with aqueous
coating; inserts: Canson Satin

RESTAURANT
One Fifth Avenue

CLIENT
Jerome Kretchmer

DESIGN FIRM
Pentagram Design

ART DIRECTORS
Paula Scher (graphics),
James Biber (interiors)

DESIGNER
Ron Louie

PHOTOGRAPHER
Peter Mauss/Esto

PAPER/PRINTING
Mohawk Superfine

ONE
FIFTH
AVENUE

NEW
YORK,
NY

10003

(212)
529-1515

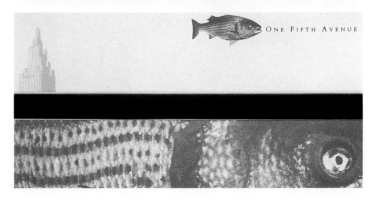

ONE FIFTH AVENUE

RESTAURANT
Shorty Small's
Great American Restaurant

DESIGN FIRM
Val Gene Associates

ART DIRECTOR/DESIGNER
Lacy Leverett

ILLUSTRATOR
Christopher Jennings

PRODUCTION
Shirley Morrow

PRINTING
Web press

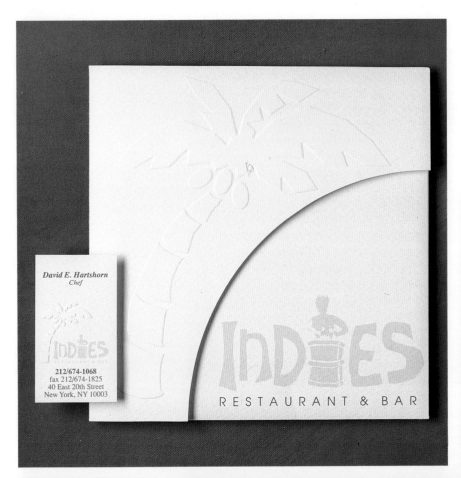

RESTAURANT/CLIENT
Indies

DESIGN FIRM
Jeff Fisher Design

ART DIRECTOR
Todd Pierce

DESIGNER/ILLUSTRATOR
Jeff Fisher

PRINTING
Harbor Graphics

Business card included a blind-embossed palm tree, also used on the menu folder. Identity was created in Macromedia FreeHand; the typeface was specially designed.

RESTAURANT
Fish Co.

CLIENTS
Michael Bank, Randy La Ferr

DESIGN FIRM
Rusty Kay & Associates

ART DIRECTOR
Rusty Kay

DESIGNER
Susan Rogers

PHOTOGRAPHER
Bill VanScoy

PRINTING
B & G Printing

CLIENT
Omni Hotels

DESIGN FIRM
Associates Design

ART DIRECTOR
Chuck Polonsky

DESIGNERS/ILLUSTRATORS
Beth Finn, Jill Arena,
Shirley Bonk, Mary Greco

Various media was used for the
creation of this project,
including oil pastels, acrylic,
marker and pencil.

RESTAURANT
Citrus

DESIGN FIRM
Bright & Associates

ART DIRECTOR
Keith Bright

DESIGNERS/ILLUSTRATORS
Peter Sargent, Wilson Ong

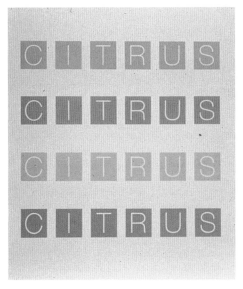

RESTAURANT
Casa Havana

CLIENT
Columbia Sussex/
Westin Casurian

DESIGN FIRM
Associates Design

ART DIRECTOR
Chuck Polonsky

DESIGNER/ILLUSTRATOR
Mary Greco

RESTAURANT
Swan Court

CLIENT
Hyatt Regency Maui

DESIGN FIRM
Associates Design

ART DIRECTOR
Chuck Polonsky

DESIGNER
Jill Arena

ILLUSTRATOR
Susan Patrtira

PAPER
Classic Linen

RESTAURANT
Oceana

CLIENT
Marriott Hotels

DESIGN FIRM
Associates Design

ART DIRECTOR
Chuck Polonsky

DESIGNER/ILLUSTRATOR
Jill Arena

PAPER
Carolina Cover

RESTAURANT/CLIENT
Riva

DESIGN FIRM
Associates Design

ART DIRECTOR
Chuck Polonsky

DESIGNER/ILLUSTRATOR
Shirley Bonk

This illustration was first created in pen and ink.

Starters

...TED GARLIC AND ASIAGO CROSTINI 6.50
...Salsa, Smoked Chicken and Melted Goat Cheese

... SEARED SCALLOPS 9.50
...Black Bean Relish and Braised Leeks

...ESE FRIED DUCK 5.95
...ola Anchovy Sauce

...NUT SHRIMP 7.95
...Red Chile Pepper Sauce

...TTERS 5.95
...h Bonnat Remoulade

...CAKE 9.30
...el Pepper Sauce

... and Fresh Tarragon,

...4.50

...7.95

...Chicken 11.95

...sa Cheese

...an BLACK BEAN SOUP 4.75
With Cilantro Sour Cream

CAYMAN CONCH CHOWDER 4.95

★ Main Courses ★

THAI SEARED TUNA $1.00
Paw Paw, Cucumber Disks, Leeks and an Onion Pancake

BLACKENED YELLOWTAIL SNAPPER $22.00
Sea Urchin Cream, Cilantro Jicama Salad

PECAN-CRUSTED WAHOO 19.50
Basmati Rice, Zucchini and Leeks

SEARED ATLANTIC SALMON $1.50
Sweet Vermouth and Lime Glaze, Spring Vegetables and Fried Potato Galette

TOP OF THE CATCH PRICED DAILY
Fresh Daily Selections May Include Grouper, Mahi Mahi, Marlin, Wahoo or Tuna

TANDOORI GRILLED MAHI 18.00
Sautéed Callaloo with Soba Noodles

PARMESAN-CRUSTED SWORDFISH 18.50
Roasted Garlic Mashed Potatoes and Braised Leeks

RUM-GRILLED SHRIMP 19.95
Yellow Tomato Jam, Coconut-Fried Potato Straws and Black Bean Salsa

BROILED GROUPER $1.00
Served with Wasabi Crème Fraîche, Roasted Balsamic Fennel and Lemon Demi Glace

CUMIN-ROASTED PORK LOIN 19.00
Seasoned with Mustard Garlic, Lime and Cilantro,
Served with Crisp Fried Potato Pancake and Apple Mango Salsa

GRILLED NEW YORK STRIP STEAK $23.00
Green Chile Garlic Sauce, Asiago Polenta and Fresh Vegetables

GRILLED FILET MIGNON $25.00
Parmesan Potato Galette, Roasted Garlic Mashed Potatoes and Pencil Asparagus

RACK OF NEW ZEALAND LAMB $6.00
Herb-Crusted with Wild Mushrooms and Sweet Corn Ragout, English Roast Potato and Mint Merlot Demi

ROASTED BREAST OF CHICKEN 18.00
Goat Cheese, Fresh Picked Basil, Straw Onions and Blackened Tomato Sauce

LEMON PEPPER FETTUCCINE 18.50
Tossed with Grilled Shrimp and Shaved Asiago Cheese, Basil and Yellow Pepper Pesto

TOMATO SAFFRON LINGUINE 16.00
Grilled Sea Bass, Mint and Orange Pesto

BAMBOO STEAMER VEGETABLE MELANGE 15.00
An Assortment of Fresh Vegetables

Desserts

PIÑA COLADA FLAN 4.50   TROPICAL FRUIT MELBA 4.50

BANANA SPLIT 5.50
With Fresh Papaya, Mango and Pineapple

FRESH BERRY NAPOLEON 4.95   FROZEN KEY LIME PIE 5.50

All Prices are Listed in Cayman Island Dollars.
A 15% Gratuity Will Be Added to Each Check. Please Refrain from Cigar or Pipe Smoking.
Half Portions are Available for Children Under Twelve at Half Price.

FERDINAND'S
C A R I B B E A N   C A F E

RESTAURANT
Ferdinand's Caribbean Cafe

CLIENT
Columbia Sussex/
Westin Casurian

DESIGN FIRM
Associates Design

ART DIRECTOR
Chuck Polonsky

DESIGNER/ILLUSTRATOR
Jill Arena

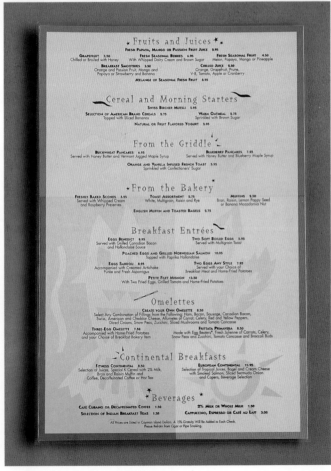

★ Fruits and Juices ★

FRESH PAPAYA, MANGO OR PASSION FRUIT JUICE 3.95

GRAPEFRUIT 3.50   FRESH SEASONAL BERRIES 6.95   FRESH SEASONAL FRUIT 4.50
Chilled or Broiled with Honey   With Whipped Dairy Cream and Brown Sugar   Melon, Papaya, Mango or Pineapple

BREAKFAST SMOOTHIES 3.50   CHILLED JUICE 3.50
Orange and Passion Fruit, Mango and   Orange, Grapefruit, Prune,
Papaya or Strawberry and Banana   V-8, Tomato, Apple or Cranberry

MELANGE OF SEASONAL FRESH FRUIT 8.95

Cereal and Morning Starters

SWISS BIRCHER MUESLI 3.50

SELECTION OF AMERICAN BRAND CEREALS 2.75   WARM OATMEAL 2.75
Topped with Sliced Bananas   Sprinkled with Brown Sugar

NATURAL OR FRUIT FLAVORED YOGURT 2.95

From the Griddle

BUCKWHEAT PANCAKES 6.95   BLUEBERRY PANCAKES 7.05
Served with Honey Butter and Vermont Jugged Maple Syrup   Served with Honey Butter and Blueberry Maple Syrup

ORANGE AND VANILLA INFUSED FRENCH TOAST 5.95
Sprinkled with Confectioners' Sugar

★ From the Bakery ★

FRESHLY BAKED SCONES 3.25   TOAST ASSORTMENT 2.75   MUFFINS 2.50
Served with Whipped Cream   White, Multigrain, Raisin and Rye   Bran, Raisin, Lemon Poppy Seed
and Raspberry Preserves   or Banana Macadamia Nut

ENGLISH MUFFIN AND TOASTED BAGELS 2.75

Breakfast Entrées

EGGS BENEDICT 8.95   TWO SOFT BOILED EGGS 5.95
Served with Grilled Canadian Bacon   Served with Multigrain Toast
and Hollandaise Sauce

POACHED EGGS AND GRILLED NORWEGIAN SALMON 10.95
Topped with Paprika Hollandaise

EGGS SARDOU 8.95   TWO EGGS ANY STYLE 7.95
Accompanied with Creamed Artichoke   Served with your Choice of
Purée and Fresh Asparagus   Breakfast Meat and Home-Fried Potatoes

PETITE FILET MIGNON 13.50
With Two Fried Eggs, Grilled Tomato and Home-Fried Potatoes

Omelettes

CREATE YOUR OWN OMELETTE 8.50
Select Any Combination of Fillings from the Following: Ham, Bacon, Sausage, Canadian Bacon,
Swiss, American and Cheddar Cheese, Allumetes of Carrot, Celery, Red and Yellow Peppers,
Diced Onions, Snow Peas, Zucchini, Sliced Mushrooms and Tomato Concasse

THREE-EGG OMELETTE 7.50   FRITTATA PRIMAVERA 8.50
Accompanied with Home-Fried Potatoes   Made with Egg Beaters®, Fresh Julienne of Carrots, Celery,
and your Choice of Breakfast Bakery Item   Snow Peas and Zucchini, Tomato Concasse and Broccoli Buds

Continental Breakfasts

FITNESS CONTINENTAL 8.50   EUROPEAN CONTINENTAL 11.95
Selection of Juices, Special K Cereal with 2% Milk,   Selection of Tropical Juices, Bagel and Cream Cheese
Bran and Raisin Muffin and   with Smoked Salmon, Sliced Bermuda Onion
Coffee, Decaffeinated Coffee or Hot Tea   and Capers, Beverage Selection

★ Beverages ★

CAFÉ CUBANO OR DECAFFEINATED COFFEE 1.50   2% MILK OR WHOLE MILK 1.50

SELECTION OF INDIAN BREAKFAST TEAS 1.50   CAPPUCCINO, ESPRESSO OR CAFÉ AU LAIT 3.00

All Prices are Listed in Cayman Island Dollars. A 15% Gratuity Will Be Added to Each Check.
Please Refrain from Cigar or Pipe Smoking.

RESTAURANT/CLIENT
Cajun Catfish Restaurant

DESIGN FIRM
GAF Advertising/Design

ART DIRECTOR/DESIGNER
Gregg A. Floyd

The catfish illustration was a pencil drawing cut in rubylith; the type was calligraphy.

RESTAURANT
Elliott's Seafood Cafe

CLIENT
Consolidated Restaurants

DESIGN FIRM
Hornall Anderson
Design Works, Inc.

ART DIRECTOR
Jack Anderson

DESIGNERS
Jack Anderson, Mary Hermes

LETTERER
Ted Wada

RESTAURANT
Ventanas Del Mar

CLIENT
Hyatt Regency Aruba

DESIGN FIRM
Associates Design

ART DIRECTOR
Chuck Polonsky

DESIGNER
Jill Arena

ILLUSTRATOR
Shirley Bonk

These illustrations were first
rendered with acrylics.

RESTAURANT/CLIENT
Frangista

DESIGN FIRM
Associates Design

ART DIRECTOR
Chuck Polonsky

DESIGNER/ILLUSTRATOR
Jill Arena

This illustration was first
created as an oil pastel.

Sports
Restaurants

Retro
Restaurants

BREAKFAST

RESTAURANT
FleetCenter

CLIENT
Sportservice

DESIGN FIRM
Associates Design

ART DIRECTOR
Chuck Polonsky

DESIGNERS
Jill Arena, Mary Greco,
Beth Finn, Shirley Bonk

ILLUSTRATOR
Jill Arena

Map and menu were
done in watercolor.

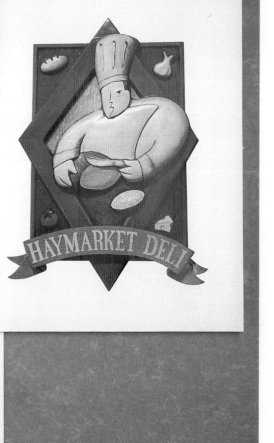

PREMIUM CLUB

WELCOME TO THE PREMIUM CLUB

The Premium Club is more than just a restaurant... it's a combination of sight and sound, aroma and taste, making dining just one part of the experience. Watch our creative chefs perform their art in front of your eyes. Sample an endless array of innovative dishes from five dining areas in an exciting marketplace atmosphere. And there's no need to miss the action on the arena floor while you enjoy your meal... it's all part of the excitement of Premium Club dining.

NORTH END PIZZERIA
A TASTE OF OLD WORLD ITALY

Mama-mia what a Pizzeria! At North End Pizzeria we make our pizza dough daily from scratch, allowing you to taste the freshness in every bite. Locally grown, hand-picked herbs and spices enhance the flavor of our savory sauce, topped with only the purest mozzarella, provolone and cheddar cheeses. Our chefs certainly create Boston's best pizzas!

PIZZAS 8.50
SUPREME – Pepperoni and Sausage
THREE CHEESE – Provolone, Mozzarella and Cheddar
MARGHERITA – Tomato and Basil
BBQ CHICKEN – Barbecue Chicken and Caramelized Onions

BOSTON GRILL
FLEETCENTER'S BACKYARD BARBECUE

Enjoy the delicious aroma of the Boston Grill as you watch our chefs prepare tender grilled beef, poultry and tuna. Boston Grill...bringing that backyard barbecue flavor to FleetCenter.

CHARBROILED SIRLOIN BURGER 7.95
Freshly Ground with American or Swiss Cheese
GRILLED CHICKEN SANDWICH 7.95
FIRE-GRILLED ITALIAN SAUSAGE 5.75
CHARBROILED TUNA SANDWICH 8.00
BIJOU TURKEY BURGER 7.50
HOMEMADE SEASONED FRIES 3.50

BACK BAY SEAFOOD
THE FRESHEST SEAFOOD IN BOSTON

Our talented chefs are always searching for the freshest seafood from the New England seas to create their special entrees. From local shrimping boats come the largest jumbo shrimp to ever hit the shore, and of course, our authentic New England clam chowder is not to be missed. For the freshest seafood in FleetCenter (not to mention Boston) visit Back Bay.

NEW ENGLAND LOBSTER SALAD ROLL 9.50
COOL JUMBO SHRIMP COCKTAIL 8.50
STEAMED CLAMS OR MUSSELS 7.50
FRIED CLAMS, SPICY TARTAR SAUCE 9.00
FRIED CALAMARI, MARINARA SAUCE 7.50
FISH AND CHIPS 9.75
CLAM CHOWDER 3.75

THE HAYMARKET DELI
FLEETCENTER'S ONE STOP PICNIC SHOP

Plan a FleetCenter picnic feast complete with all the fixings at the Haymarket Deli. Finish your made-to-order sandwich with an assortment of gourmet toppings and one of our many side dishes. Stop by Haymarket Deli today and pick up a picnic.

SANDWICHES 7.50
Carved Roast Round of Beef, Broiled Turkey Breast or Virginia Smoked
Ham Sandwich with Choice of Gourmet Toppings and Side Dish
GRILLED CHICKEN CAESAR SALAD 6.50
ANTIPASTO PLATE 7.25
CHEF SALAD 6.50

DOLCI'S SWEET TOOTH
SWEETS TO PLEASE

Sweet temptations become a reality at Dolci's. Our bakers are masters at creating spectacular desserts to satisfy the sweetest of cravings. Creamy, hand-whipped cream cheese frosting adds a rich flavor to the moist, layered carrot cake. Fresh fruit fills the light, flaky crust of our tarts and the white chocolate-layered raspberry cheesecake is made with only the finest chocolate and richest whipped cheese. Stop by Dolci's for a sweet to please every craving!

WHITE CHOCOLATE
RASPBERRY CHEESECAKE 4.50
CHOCOLATE PECAN MOUSSE 4.50
FRESH FRUIT TART 4.50
CARROT CAKE 4.50
TIRAMISU 4.50
SOFT SERVE ICE CREAM AND YOGURT 3.95
With Assorted Toppings
FUDGE BROWNIES 2.50
White and Dark Chocolate Gourmet Brownies
FRESHLY BAKED COOKIES 2.00
Chocolate Chip, Oatmeal Raisin
and White Chocolate Macadamia Nut
REGULAR AND DECAFFEINATED COFFEE 2.00
GOURMET FLAVORED COFFEES 2.00
ESPRESSO 2.50
CAPPUCCINO 3.00
CAFE LATTE 3.00
ICED CAPPUCCINO 3.00

RESTAURANT
Courtside Club

CLIENT
Sportservice

DESIGN FIRM
Associates Design

ART DIRECTOR
Chuck Polonsky

DESIGNER/ILLUSTRATOR
Beth Finn

PAPER
Insert: UV Ultra

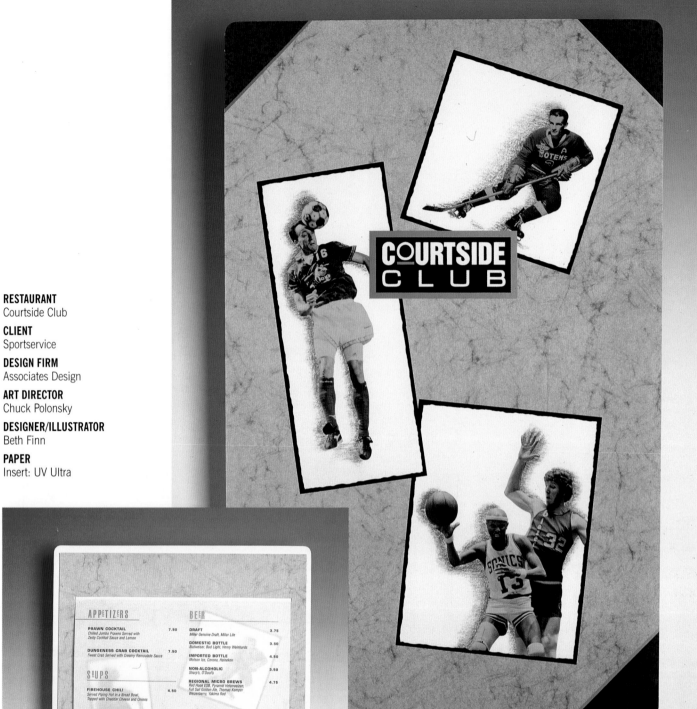

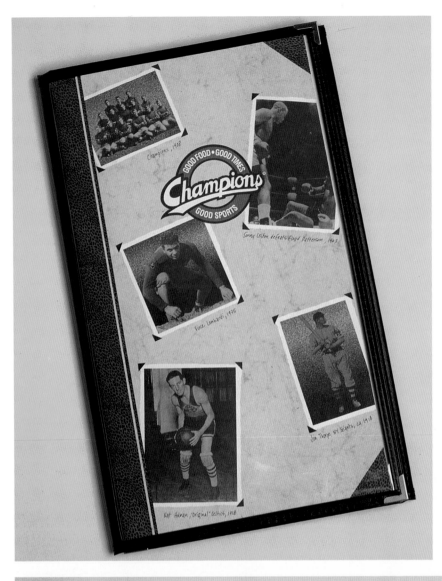

RESTAURANT
Champions

CLIENT
Marriott International

DESIGN FIRM
Associates Design

ART DIRECTOR
Chuck Polonsky

DESIGNERS
Beth Finn, Mary Greco

PAPER/PRINTING
French Speckletone

CLIENT
Sportservice

DESIGN FIRM
Associates Design

ART DIRECTOR
Chuck Polonsky

DESIGNER
Jill Arena

PAPER
Carolina Cover

RESTAURANT
KeyArena

CLIENT
Sportservice

DESIGN FIRM
Associates Design

ART DIRECTOR
Chuck Polonsky

DESIGNER
Beth Finn

RESTAURANT
Legends, FleetCenter

CLIENT
Sportservice

DESIGN FIRM
Associates Design

ART DIRECTOR
Chuck Polonsky

DESIGNER/ILLUSTRATOR
Mary Greco

PAPER
Simpson Quest

Hand-colored photos with
colored pencils.

LEGENDS

RESTAURANT
Buffalo Bills Catering Concepts

CLIENT
Sportservice

DESIGN FIRM
Associates Design

ART DIRECTOR
Chuck Polonsky

DESIGNER
Mary Greco

RESTAURANT
Banners, FleetCenter

CLIENT
Sportservice

DESIGN FIRM
Associates Design

ART DIRECTOR
Chuck Polonsky

DESIGNER
Beth Finn

PAPER
Linen

RESTAURANT
Chevy's

CLIENT
John Wiley

DESIGN FIRM
Raven Madd Design Company

ART DIRECTOR/DESIGNER
Mark Curtis

ILLUSTRATORS
Mark Curtis, Caroline Campbell

RESTAURANT
Terrace Club at Jacobs Field

CLIENT
Cleveland Indians

DESIGN FIRM
The Levy Restaurants

CREATIVE DIRECTOR
Marcy L. Young

DESIGNER
Karen Hoey

RESTAURANTS
The Stadium Club,
Mezzanine Box Catering

CLIENT
Chicago Cubs

DESIGN FIRM
The Levy Restaurants

CREATIVE DIRECTOR
Marcy L. Young

DESIGNERS
Marcy L. Young, Karen Hoey

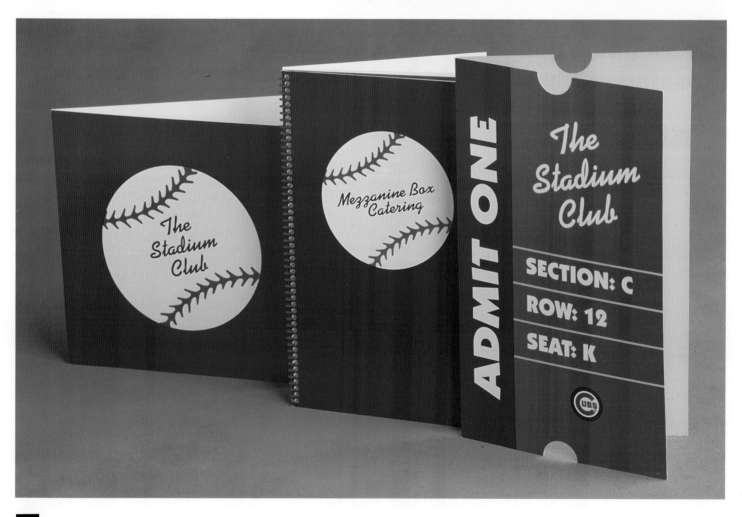

RESTAURANT
Arrowhead Club
at Arrowhead Stadium

CLIENT
Kansas City Chiefs

DESIGN FIRM
The Levy Restaurants

CREATIVE DIRECTOR
Marcy L. Young

DESIGNER
Karen Hoey

RESTAURANTS
The Rotunda, Executive Suites,
Day of Event Menu

CLIENT
Portland Trailblazers

DESIGN FIRM
The Levy Restaurants

CREATIVE DIRECTOR
Marcy L. Young

DESIGNER
Karen Hoey

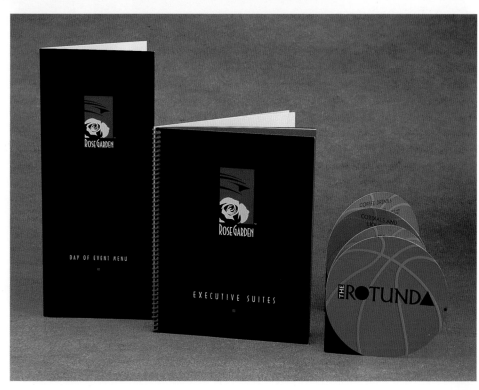

RESTAURANT
Route 66 Roadhouse
& Dining Saloon

CLIENTS
George Korten, Martin Winkler,
Kent Selig

DESIGN FIRM
Pentagram Design

ART DIRECTORS
Michael Bierut (graphics),
James Biber (interiors)

DESIGNER
Emily Hayes

PHOTOGRAPHER
Peter Mauss/Esto

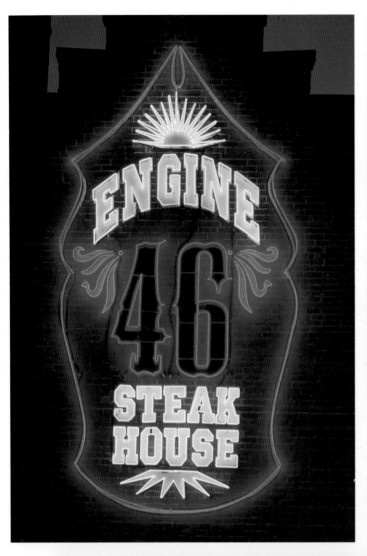

RESTAURANT/CLIENT
Engine 46 Steakhouse

DESIGN FIRM
Hanson Associates, Inc.

ART DIRECTOR
Gil Hanson

DESIGNER
Mike Welsh

PHOTOGRAPHER
Fireman's Museum

The icon was derived from
antique helmet insignias.

RESTAURANT
Beau Nash

CLIENT
Hotel Crescent Court,
Rosewood Hotels

DESIGN FIRM
David Carter Design

ART DIRECTOR/DESIGNER
Sharon LeJeune

ILLUSTRATOR
Mark Chickinelli

The inserts were laser
printed on different brightly
colored sheets so the menu
could be easily updated.

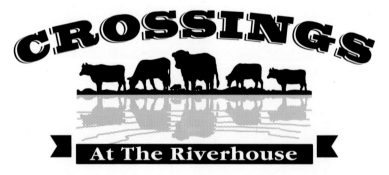

RESTAURANT
Crossings

CLIENT
The Riverhouse Resort/
Triad (Agency)

DESIGN FIRM
Jeff Fisher Design

ALL DESIGN
Jeff Fisher

The identity was created in
Macromedia FreeHand.

RESTAURANT/CLIENT
Harlow's Modern Italian

DESIGN FIRM
Page Design, Inc.

DESIGNER
Laurel Bigley Mathe

ILLUSTRATOR
Laura Zugzda

PAPER/PRINTING
80 lb. cover, gloss white

After a detailed sketch
was created, the
logo was drawn using
a Power Macintosh
and Adobe Illustrator.

RESTAURANT
Brooklyn Diner

CLIENT
Cafe Concepts

DESIGN FIRM
Russek Advertising

ART DIRECTOR/DESIGNER
Hal Jannen

ILLUSTRATOR
Martha Lewis

PAPER/PRINTING
100 lb. Lustro Dulltext,
Indigo print

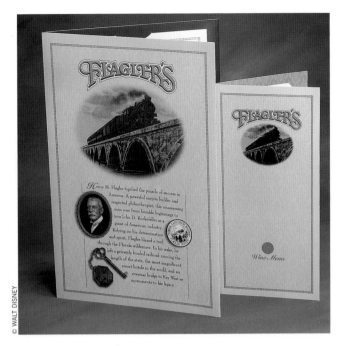

© WALT DISNEY

RESTAURANT
Flagler's

CLIENT
Disney's Grand Floridian
Beach Resort

DESIGN FIRM
Disney Design Group

ART DIRECTORS
Jeff Morris, Renée Schneider

DESIGNER
Bob Holden

WRITER
Tony Fernandez

ILLUSTRATOR
Robert Vann

PHOTOGRAPHER
Flagler Museum archives

PAPER/PRINTING
Quintessence Remarque,
4-color process, laminated,
die cut

RESTAURANT/CLIENT
Sammy's At The Arena

DESIGN FIRM
Kapp & Associates, Inc.

ART DIRECTOR
Cathryn Kapp

DESIGNERS
Derek Oyen, Sally Biel

PAPER
Vintage Velvet

All art was created using
Macromedia FreeHand.

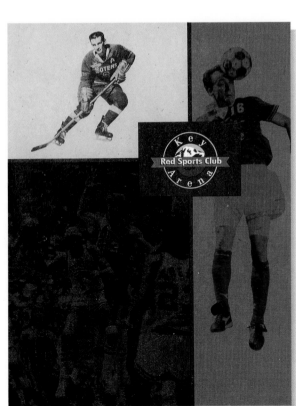

World Flavors

RESTAURANT
Cathay Pacific Inflight

CLIENT
Cathay Pacific Airways

DESIGN FIRM
PPA Design Limited

ART DIRECTOR
Byron Jacobs

DESIGNERS
Byron Jacobs, Bernard Cau

PAPER/PRINTING
Recycled paper,
offset and letterpress

Australian Aboriginal
cave paintings were used
as visual thread.

RESTAURANT
Cathay Pacific Inflight

CLIENT
Cathay Pacific Airways

DESIGN FIRM
PPA Design Limited

ART DIRECTOR/DESIGNER
Byron Jacobs

PHOTOGRAPHER
Chuck Shotwell

PAPER/PRINTING
Japanese White A; card, offset

This design merges the best
elements of East and West.

RESTAURANT
Cathay Pacific Inflight

CLIENT
Cathay Pacific Airways

DESIGN FIRM
PPA Design Limited

ART DIRECTOR
Byron Jacobs

DESIGNERS
Byron Jacobs, Tracy Hoi

PHOTOGRAPHER
Ka Sing Lee

PAPER/PRINTING
Japanese White A Card, offset

Each menu portrays one of the
Five Elements of Nature in
Chinese religious beliefs: water,
metal, wood, fire and earth.

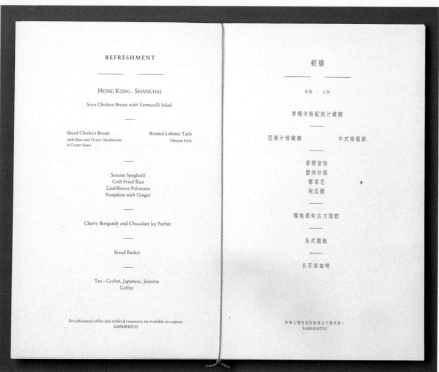

RESTAURANT
Dragon Airlines Inflight

CLIENT
Dragon Airlines

DESIGN FIRM
PPA Design Limited

ART DIRECTOR
Byron Jacobs

DESIGNERS
Byron Jacobs, Don Funk

ILLUSTRATOR
Brian Grimwood

PAPER/PRINTING
Japanese White A, offset

RESTAURANT
La Serre

CLIENT
Sylvain Fareri

DESIGN FIRM
Louise Fili Ltd.

ART DIRECTOR/DESIGNER
Louise Fili

La Serre is French for "greenhouse." The printing is on cream parchment.

RESTAURANT/CLIENT
Espace

DESIGN FIRM
Louise Fili Ltd.

ALL DESIGN
Louise Fili

RESTAURANT
Rosey Tomatoes

DESIGN FIRM
Louise Fili Ltd.

ART DIRECTOR/DESIGNER
Louise Fili

ILLUSTRATOR
Melanie Parks

PAPER/PRINTING
One-size sticker: on recycled Hopper Proterra stock

RESTAURANT
Vivaldi Ristorante Italiano

CLIENT
Vivaldi

ART DIRECTOR/DESIGNER
Hector Di Luzio

The project's original
CMYK colors were replaced
by the logo's spot colors.

RESTAURANT/CLIENT
Stella D'Italia Restaurant

DESIGN FIRM
Bullet Communications Inc.

ALL DESIGN
Tim Scott

The "stella" logo lettering
was hand-drawn. The business
card was printed using
PMS 342 green with gold foil
hot-stamping.

RESTAURANT
Equator

CLIENT
Caneel Bay—Rosewood Hotels

DESIGN FIRM
David Carter Design

ART DIRECTOR
Lori B. Wilson

DESIGNER
Tracy Huck

ILLUSTRATOR
Mary King

PAPER
Starwhite Vicksburg

RESTAURANT
Bansai

CLIENT
Hyatt Regency Osaka

DESIGN FIRM
David Carter Design

ART DIRECTOR/DESIGNER
Sharon LeJeune

ILLUSTRATOR
Susan Miller

PAPER/PRINTING
Corrugated plastic

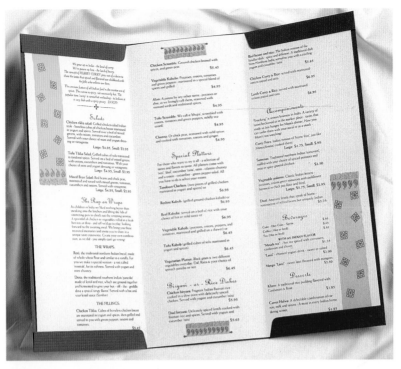

RESTAURANT/CLIENT
Hurry Curry

DESIGN FIRM
Mehul Design

ART DIRECTOR/DESIGNER
Mehul Parekh

PAPER/PRINTING
Neenah Environment
& Cover, Beckett, Ridge/
3-color spot printing

The fabric illustration
was drawn in Adobe Illustrator;
the menu layout and type
was done in QuarkXPress; the
inside shells of menus
were pre-printed, 2-color.

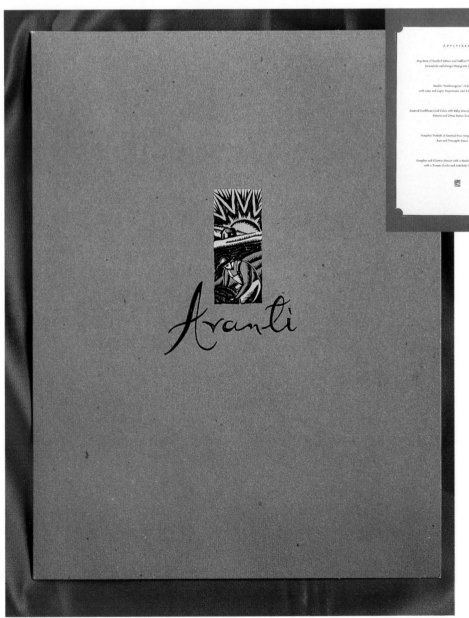

RESTAURANT
Avanti

CLIENT
The Princeton Dubai

DESIGN FIRM
David Carter Design

ART DIRECTOR/DESIGNER
Gary Lobue, Jr.

ILLUSTRATOR
Tracy Huck

A registered, dull-foil stamp
over a 4-color process
illustration mimics a woodcut
engraving. Inserts are laser-
printed daily by the client.

RESTAURANT
Amapola

CLIENT
Hotel Principe Felipe

DESIGN FIRM
David Carter Design

ART DIRECTOR/DESIGNER
Lori B. Wilson

ILLUSTRATORS
Local Spanish children

PAPER
Simpson Quest

Amapola means "poppy"
in Spanish, so the graphic for
the menu incorporates a
stylized poppy with a wrought-
iron feeling, which relates
to the interior architecture of
the restaurant.

RESTAURANT
Star Canyon

DESIGN FIRM
David Carter Design

ART DIRECTOR/DESIGNER
Gary Lobue, Jr.

ILLUSTRATORS
Ed Patton, Gary Lobue, Jr.

PAPER/PRINTING
Dull laminate, debossed
area with tip-on
that is interchangeable

Laser print-outs are inserted
into the menu daily.

APPETIZERS
Almond Baked Brie with Dried Fruit Compote $4.50
Smoked Salmon Nachos with Guacamole and Caviar Cream $7.25
Mozzarella on Spinach Leaves with Vinaigrette $8.25
Fried Calamari with Saffron Aioli and Roasted Tomato Sauce $5.50
Corn Fritters with Roasted Peanut-Cucumber Relish $6.00
Turkey Dumplings with Mushroom Broth $6.50

SOUP & SALADS
Star Canyon Grilled Corn and Smoked Chicken Soup $4.50
Ranch Chili with Jalapeno Corn Bread $4.75
Star Canyon House Salad with Herbal Vinaigrette $6.50
Caesar Salad with Maytag Blue Cheese $4.75
Tortilla Salad With Bean Cakes and Jalapeno Dressing $7.50
Greek Salad with Chicken and Oregano $8.50

DINNER PLATES
Alaskan Salmon with Bok Choy and Mushrooms $28.50
Louisiana Crab Cakes with Wilted Spinach and Tomato Vinaigrette $22.75
Cabbage and Potato Casserole with Green Bean Stroganoff $9.00
Texas T-Bone with Green Chili Scalloped Potatoes and BBQ Beans $18.50
Roast Chicken with Tuscan Bread and Sun Dried Tomatoes $14.50

DESSERTS
Selection of Desserts $7.50

Please Refrain from Pipe and Cigar Smoking. Thank You.

RESTAURANT
Zest Cantina

CLIENT
Hasegawa Enterprise Ltd.

DESIGN FIRM
Vrontikis Design Office

ART DIRECTOR
Petrula Vrontikis

DESIGNER
Kim Sage

ILLUSTRATOR
Christina Hsiao

PAPER/PRINTING
Simpson Quest

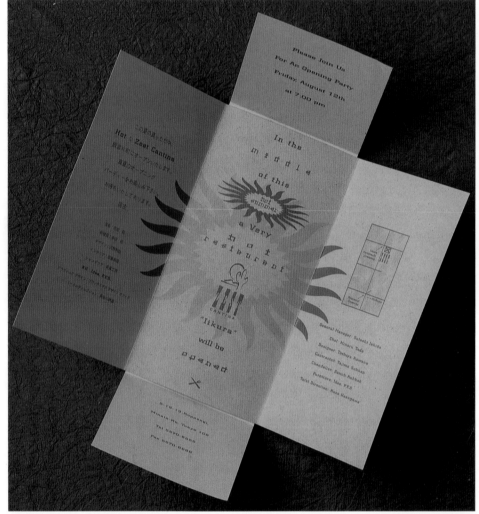

RESTAURANT
Cafe La Boheme

CLIENT
Hasegawa Enterprise Ltd.

DESIGN FIRM
Vrontikis Design Office

ART DIRECTOR
Petrula Vrontikis

DESIGNER
Kim Sage

RESTAURANT
Jacksons

CLIENT
Alan Jackson

DESIGN FIRM
Vrontikis Design Office

ART DIRECTOR
Petrula Vrontikis

DESIGNER
Kim Sage

PAPER/PRINTING
Speckletone

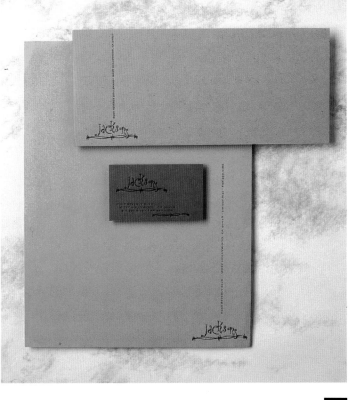

RESTAURANT
Reginelli's

CLIENTS
Darryl Reginelli,
Stephanie Bruno

DESIGN FIRM
Zande Newman Design

DESIGNERS
Michelle Zande,
Adam Newman

ILLUSTRATOR
Robert Guthrie

PAPER
Cover, Kimdura; inside pages,
French Speckletone, Natural;
daily specials, Quest, Bronze

Three different paintbrushes
indicate brunch, lunch
or dinner menus. Insides
laid out in QuarkXPress
allow menu contents
to change every season.

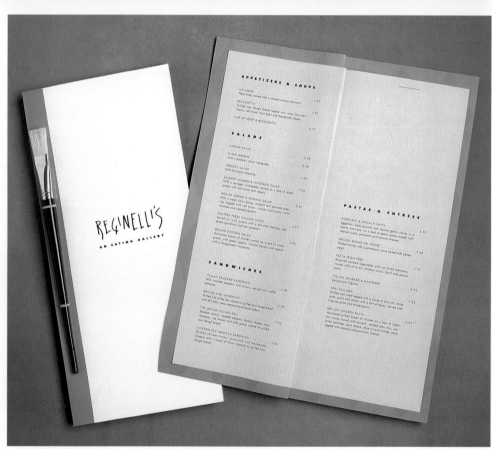

RESTAURANT
Maria's Cucina

CLIENT
Boris Brezinger

DESIGN FIRM
Artie Horowitz Design

ALL DESIGN
Artie Horowitz

PRINTING
Pyramid Press

This project was entirely hand-illustrated.

TEXANNA RED'S WALKIN'

RESTAURANT
Texanna Red's

DESIGN FIRM
Val Gene Associates

ART DIRECTOR/DESIGNER
Lacy Leverett

APPETIZERS

GUACAMOLE DIP $3.95
A traditional Mexican favorite made fresh daily in Red's kitchen.

LAYERED DIP $4.95
Refried beans, guacamole, pico de gallo, hot sauce and cheese baked in a casserole served with flour tortillas

CHEESE NACHOS $5.25
Plenty of light corn chips covered with Cheddar and Monterey Jack cheeses, topped with jalapeño slices.

BEAN NACHOS $5.50
Our Cheese Nachos loaded with plenty of refried beans and jalapeños.

SPICY BEEF NACHOS $6.25
Texanna Red's Cheese Nachos covered with taco beef and jalapeño peppers.

CHICKEN NACHOS $6.50
Texanna Red's Cheese Nachos topped with spicy chicken, sour cream, jalapeño peppers and black olives.

CALIENTITAS $4.95
Spicy jalapeño peppers filled with cream cheese, then breaded and deep-fried to a golden brown.

CHICKEN FLAUTAS $4.95
Corn tortillas filled with spicy chicken then deep-fried, served with sour cream.

QUESO DIP $2.95
Spicy cheese dip.

TEXADINNERS

FILET $13.95
An 8-ounce, mesquite-broiled beef tenderloin, served with salad and Texas toast.

STRIP STEAK $13.25
A 10-ounce, mesquite-broiled Kansas City strip steak, served with salad and Texas toast

TEXANNA CHICKEN $7.25
A large marinated chicken breast, mesquite-broiled with marinated onions, topped with Monterey Jack cheese; served oven-faced on Texas toast

CHICKEN FRIED STEAK DINNER $7.25
A traditional Southwest favorite! Served with country gravy, a dinner salad and Texas toast

BROILED CHICKEN WITH SOUR CREAM SAUCE $7.25
A large mesquite-broiled chicken breast topped with Red's own sour cream sauce and Monterey Jack cheese; served with Mexican rice and refried beans

SANTA FE CHICKEN $7.25
Mesquite-broiled chicken breast covered with barbecued onions, black olives, green onions, mixed cheeses and diced tomatoes; served with Mexican rice and refried beans.

RED'S FIESTA PLATTER

A COMBINATION OF HOUSE FAVORITES $8.95
Two jumbo enchiladas (1 beef, 1 chicken), two tacos (1 beef, 1 chicken), one calientita, cheese nachos and fresh guacamole; served with rice and beans

MESQUITE-BROILED BURGERS
Burgers are accompanied by French fries.

MESQUITE BURGER $4.95
With lettuce, tomato, pickle and onion.

MESQUITE BURGER WITH CHEESE $5.45
With lettuce, tomato, pickle, cheese and onion.

QUESO BURGER $5.65
With hot queso, sour cream and chives.

GUACAMOLE AND JACK CHEESE BURGER $5.65
With lettuce and tomato.

HICKORY BURGER $5.65
With Red's hickory sauce, Cheddar cheese, pickles and mayo.

TEXANNA'S SALADS

SOMBRERO SALAD $6.25
A large flour tortilla shell filled with lettuce, taco beef, cheese, guacamole, sour cream, chopped tomato and black olives; topped with Red's house dressing.

CHEF SALAD $5.95
A large flour tortilla shell filled with lettuce, ham, mesquite-broiled chicken breast, cheese, chopped tomato and black olives; served with the dressing of your choice

HOT FAJITA SALAD $6.75
A large flour tortilla shell filled with lettuce, tomatoes, and black olives; topped with your choice of tender hot strips of chicken or beef, then sprinkled with Cheddar and Jack cheeses.

DINNER SALAD $2.25
Features salad greens, chopped tomato and cheese

RED'S BURNERS
Served with Mexican rice and refried beans.

CHILI RITO $5.95
A combination of beans, lettuce and tomatoes' rolled in a flour tortilla; topped with chili con carne and hot queso.

BEEF CHIMICHANGA $6.50
A large flour tortilla filled with spicy beef, lettuce and chopped tomato, then deep-fried topped with rancheria sauce, melted cheese and guacamole.

CHICKEN CHIMICHANGA $6.50
A large flour tortilla filled with spicy chicken, lettuce and diced tomato then deep-fried; topped with sour cream sauce and melted Monterey Jack cheese.

RED'S BURRITO (Chicken or Beef) $5.95
Your choice of spicy beef or spicy chicken with beans, lettuce and tomato rolled in a large flour tortilla; topped with rancheria sauce and cheese (Red's chicken burrito is topped with sour cream sauce.)

BEEF OR CHICKEN CHALUPA $5.50
A flour tortilla shell filled with taco beef or spicy chicken, lettuce, cheese and tomatoes; topped with guacamole and black olives (Red's chicken chalupa is topped with sour cream.)

TOSTADAS $5.75
Our three tostadas: beef, chicken and bean; topped with cheese, lettuce, tomatoes, sour cream, guacamole and black olives. (Not served with beans and rice.)

CHILI RELLENOS (1) $6.25 (2) $7.50
We take a mild green chile, stuff it with your choice of beef or cheese, then we deep-fry it and top it with rancheria sauce and chopped tomatoes.

TEXANNA'S SPECIALTIES

SIZZLING FAJITAS (FA-HE-TAS) Marinated chicken or beef strips grilled over mesquite wood then served sizzling on a cast iron platter with marinated onion rings.

SIZZLING BEEF FAJITAS
Small Order . . . . $8.95 Large Order $15.95
A marinated, mesquite-broiled steak sliced into strips, accompanied by marinated onions, guacamole, pico de gallo and flour tortillas.

SIZZLING CHICKEN FAJITAS
Small Order . . . . $8.95 Large Order $15.95
Marinated, mesquite-broiled chicken breast sliced into strips, served with marinated onions, sour cream, guacamole, cheese, pico de gallo and flour tortillas.

SIZZLING SHRIMP FAJITAS
Small Order . . . . $9.95 Large Order $15.95
Marinated, mesquite-broiled shrimp, served with marinated onions, guacamole, sour cream, cheese, pico de gallo and flour tortillas.

MEXICAN SPECIALTIES

These large combination dinners are served with Mexican rice and refried beans – guaranteed to satisfy even the heartiest appetite.
Any 2 Items . . . . $6.25 Any 3 Items $7.50

BEEF OR CHEESE ENCHILADAS
with chili con carne.

CHICKEN ENCHILADAS
with sour cream sauce.

BEEF OR CHICKEN TACO

SOFT CHEESE TACO
topped with queso

BORDER ORDERS

Mexican Rice	$1.50
Refried Beans	$1.50
French Fries	$1.25
Guacamole	$1.95
Sour Cream	.95
4 Soft Tortillas	.95
4 Corn Tortillas	.95
Quart of Sauce with chips to go	$4.95
Taco	$1.50
Enchilada	$2.25
Relleno	$3.25

ANNADELIGHTS

TEXANNA'S CARAMEL APPLE PIE $3.25
A large deep-fried tortilla filled with spiced apples, topped with vanilla ice cream & melted caramel.

SOPAPILLAS (2) $1.45 (4) $2.25

FRIED ICE CREAM $3.25
Fresh vanilla ice cream batter-dipped, quick-fried, and sprinkled with cinnamon and sugar; topped with peach sauce.

ALL YOU CAN EAT LUNCH BUFFET
Monday - Friday, 11 am - 2 pm
(Available for dine-in only)
$5.99

TRY RED'S CLUB
2 - 7 pm & 10:30 - 1:00 a.m.
(The following specials are offered)
2 - 7 pm & 10:30 - 1:00 a.m. everyday except Sunday
from 2 pm-7 pm only)

Free Games   Free Munchies
$2.50 - $5 oz. Draft Beer

MESOAMERICAN
CUISINE

RESTAURANT/CLIENT
Oaxaca Grill

DESIGN FIRM
Greteman Group

ART DIRECTOR
Sonia Greteman

DESIGNERS
Sonia Greteman, Jo Quillin,
Chris Parks

PAPER
Kimdura Buckskin

The metal, riveted band was rusted and coated with urethane. Logo is debossed and inks are metallic copper.

RESTAURANT
Betelnut

CLIENT
Real Restaurants

DESIGN FIRM
Russell Leong Design

ART DIRECTOR/DESIGNER
Russell Leong

Components of the logo were scanned, modified, and embellished on the computer, output on a laser printer, then photocopied many times to achieve the distressed effect. Deep red and gold were used because in Chinese culture, these indicate good luck.

RESTAURANT/CLIENT
Wok King Chinese Cuisine

DESIGN FIRM
Wicky's Graphics

ALL DESIGN
Wicky W. Lee

This logo was created in Macromedia FreeHand.

RESTAURANT/CLIENT
The Plaza Restaurant

DESIGN FIRM
Wicky's Graphics

ART DIRECTOR/DESIGNER
Wicky W. Lee

This logo was created in Adobe Illustrator; the peacock comes from a Chinese clip art book; the calligraphy is Ming Dynasty style.

RESTAURANT/CLIENT
Legend Hotel

DESIGN FIRM
Brillbank Creative
Consultants Sdn. Bhd.

ART DIRECTOR
Rayven Ho

DESIGNER
Tony Lim

PHOTOGRAPHER
C.M. Ho

RESTAURANT/CLIENT
Lu Cuisine

DESIGN FIRM
WTS Studios

DESIGNER/ILLUSTRATOR
William Silvers

A subtle logo, this was
designed to resemble
the brushed aluminum
used in the restaurant.

RESTAURANT
Wholé Molé

CLIENT
Cornerstone Management

DESIGN FIRM
Associates Design

ART DIRECTOR
Chuck Polonsky

DESIGNER
Mary Greco

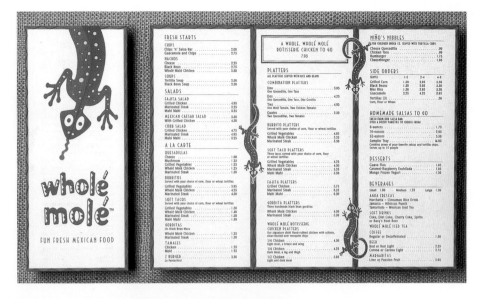

CLIENT
Omni Hotels

DESIGN FIRM
Associates Design

ART DIRECTOR
Chuck Polonsky

DESIGNER/ILLUSTRATOR
Jill Arena

PAPER
French Speckletone

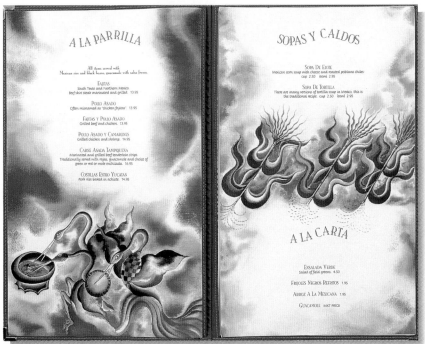

RESTAURANT/CLIENT
Fonda San Miguel

DESIGN FIRM
The Menu Workshop

ART DIRECTOR/DESIGNER
Liz Kearney

ILLUSTRATOR
Arnulfo Mendoza

PAPER/PRINTING
Color copies

RESTAURANT
Primo's

CLIENT
U.S. Army

DESIGN FIRM
Associates Design

ART DIRECTOR
Chuck Polonsky

DESIGNER/ILLUSTRATOR
Jill Arena

PAPER
French Speckletone True White

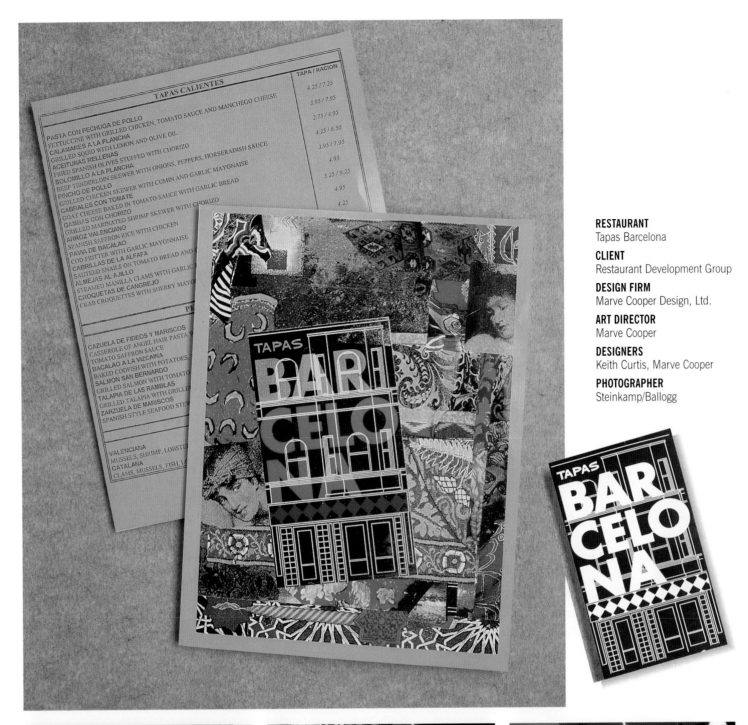

TAPAS CALIENTES

	TAPA / RACION
	4.25 / 7.25
PASTA CON PECHUGA DE POLLO	3.95 / 7.95
FETTUCCINE WITH GRILLED CHICKEN, TOMATO SAUCE AND MANCHEGO CHEESE	2.75 / 4.95
CALAMARES A LA PLANCHA	
GRILLED SQUID WITH LEMON AND OLIVE OIL	4.25 / 8.50
ACEITUNAS RELLENAS	
FRIED SPANISH OLIVES STUFFED WITH CHORIZO	3.95 / 7.95
SOLOMILLO A LA PLANCHA	
BEEF TENDERLOIN SKEWER WITH ONIONS, PEPPERS, HORSERADISH SAUCE	4.95
PINCHO DE POLLO	
GRILLED CHICKEN SKEWER WITH CUMIN AND GARLIC MAYONAISE	5.25 / 9.25
CABRALES CON TOMATE	
GOAT CHEESE BAKED IN TOMATO SAUCE WITH GARLIC BREAD	4.95
GAMBAS CON CHORIZO	
GRILLED MARINATED SHRIMP SKEWER WITH CHORIZO	4.25
ARROZ VALENCIANO	
SPANISH SAFFRON RICE WITH CHICKEN	
PAVIA DE BACALAO	
COD FRITTER WITH GARLIC MAYONNAISE	
CABRILLAS DE LA ALFAFA	
SAUTEED SNAILS ON TOMATO BREAD AND G	
ALMEJAS AL AJILLO	
STEAMED MANILLA CLAMS WITH GARLIC	
CROQUETAS DE CANGREJO	
CRAB CROQUETTES WITH SHERRY MAYO	

PE

CAZUELA DE FIDEOS Y MARISCOS
CASSEROLE OF ANGEL HAIR PASTA W
TOMATO SAFFRON SAUCE
BACALAO A LA VIZCAINA
BAKED CODFISH WITH POTATOES,
SALMON SAN BERNARDO
GRILLED SALMON WITH TOMATO
TALAPIA DE LAS RAMBLAS
GRILLED TALAPIA WITH GRILLE
ZARZUELA DE MARISCOS
SPANISH STYLE SEAFOOD STEW

VALENCIANA
MUSSELS, SHRIMP, LOBSTE
CATALANA
CLAMS, MUSSELS, FISH, L

RESTAURANT
Tapas Barcelona

CLIENT
Restaurant Development Group

DESIGN FIRM
Marve Cooper Design, Ltd.

ART DIRECTOR
Marve Cooper

DESIGNERS
Keith Curtis, Marve Cooper

PHOTOGRAPHER
Steinkamp/Ballogg

RESTAURANT
Italian Oasis
Restaurant & Brewery

CLIENTS
Wayne and Lisa Morello

DESIGN FIRM
Glen Group
Marketing and Advertising

ART DIRECTOR
Maureen Rupprecht

DESIGNER/ILLUSTRATOR
Jodie Neal

Laid out in QuarkXPress,
printed through
Indigo filmless printing.

RESTAURANT
Mister Sheik

CLIENT
Central Mister Sheik

DESIGN FIRM
AWG Graphics Bureau
E Consult. Inf. Ltda.

ART DIRECTOR/DESIGNER
Renata Claudia De Cristofaro

This project was created
in CorelDRAW.

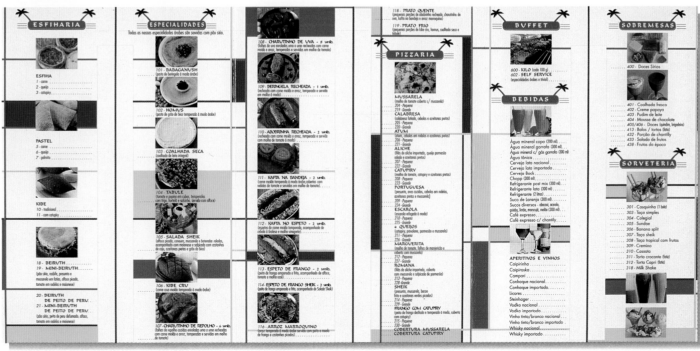

RESTAURANT
Max Amoré

CLIENT
Max Restaurant Group

DESIGN FIRM
Rainwater Design

ALL DESIGN
Jane Rainwater

PHOTOGRAPHER
Vintage photographs,
personal collection

PAPER/PRINTING
Crosspointe Genesis

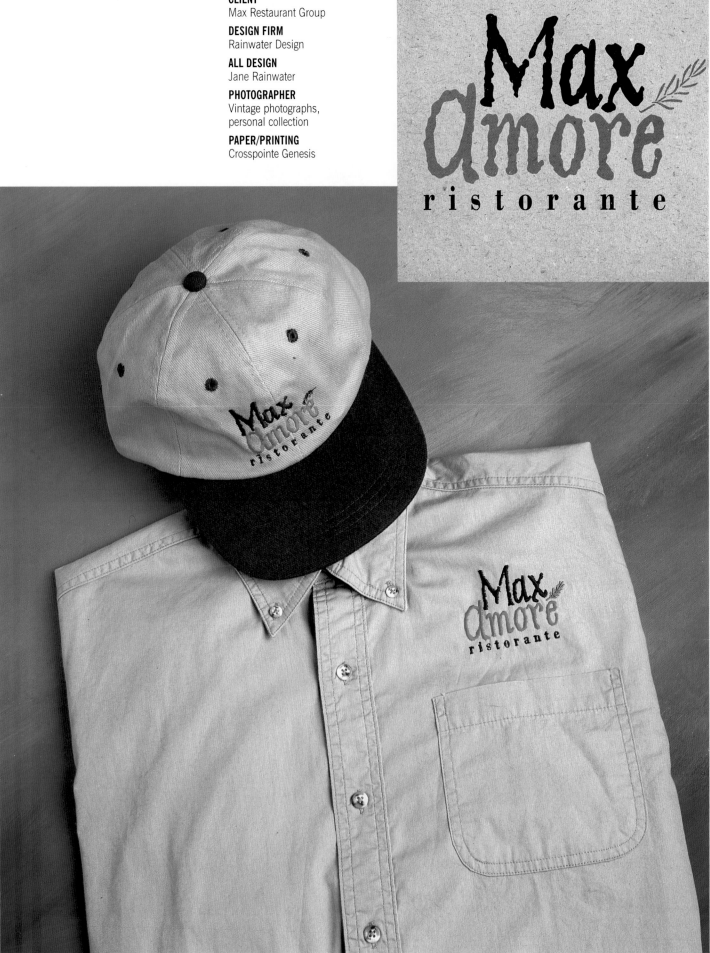

RESTAURANT
Mondo Cucina,
Wellington, New Zealand

CLIENTS
Simon, John, Kerry

DESIGNER/ILLUSTRATOR
Emma Main

PHOTOGRAPHER
Kerry MacKay

TYPESETTER
Alistair Best

SIGNAGE SCULPTORS
Andrew "Floppy" Beattie,
Peter Hutchinson

PAPER/PRINTING
Mataura Falls Bond Laid,
50% recycled paper

(Below left) An original illustration
was rendered in charcoal with ink
overlay; the illustration reflects the
restaurant's "rough" Italian cuisine
and bar.

(Below right) A "chunky"
sculpture modeled from the
Mondo Cucina logo is colored in
silver and beaten copper. The fork
is aluminum. The restaurant name
is hand-stencilled and cut on
stained wood.

(Right) The logo line art was
reversed and printed in a shade
of blue similar to the exterior of
the restaurant. A computer-
manipulated photograph of logo
sculpture of the restaurant façade
was used for both menus with
color change-out. Blank menus
were then photocopied with
appropriate details, laminated,
and folded.

MONDO-CUCINA

15 Blair Street • PO Box 6300 • Wellington • Telephone 801 6615

RESTAURANT
Park Hyatt
Johannesburg Banquet

CLIENT
Park Hyatt Johannesburg

DESIGN FIRM
HBA International / Graphis

ART DIRECTOR/DESIGNER
Kevin Scholberg

RESTAURANT/CLIENT
The Nile

DESIGN FIRM
Tony Murcia Designs

ART DIRECTOR/DESIGNER
Tony Murcia

PAPER/PRINTING
Natural papyrus, textured stock,
laser and screen printing

Designs were done in
Macromedia FreeHand.
Printing was a combination
of laser printing, inkjet,
and screen printing
on natural papyrus and cloth.
Laced binding.

RESTAURANT/CLIENT
801 Steak & Chop House

DESIGN FIRM
Sayles Graphic Design

ALL DESIGN
John Sayles

PHOTOGRAPHER
Bill Nellans

RESTAURANT
Hurry Curry

CLIENT
Michael Bank, Randy La Ferr

DESIGN FIRM
Rusty Kay & Associates

ART DIRECTOR
Rusty Kay

DESIGNER
Randall Momii

PHOTOGRAPHER
Bill VanScoy

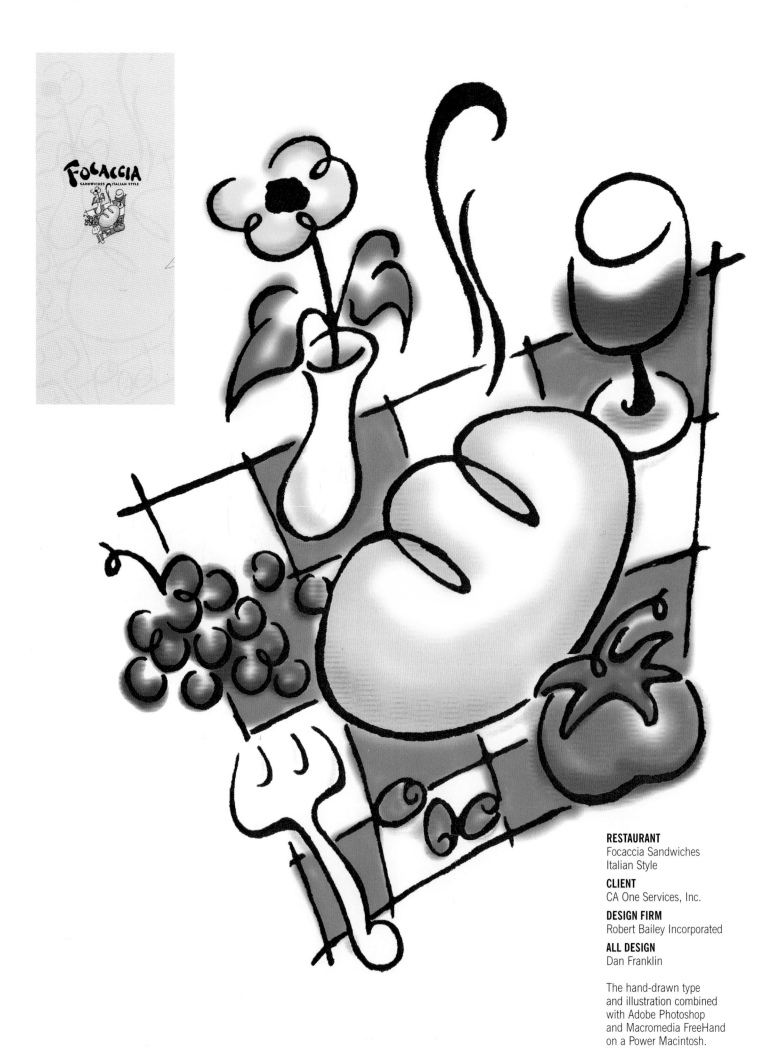

RESTAURANT
Focaccia Sandwiches
Italian Style

CLIENT
CA One Services, Inc.

DESIGN FIRM
Robert Bailey Incorporated

ALL DESIGN
Dan Franklin

The hand-drawn type
and illustration combined
with Adobe Photoshop
and Macromedia FreeHand
on a Power Macintosh.

RESTAURANT
Americo's Pizzeria

CLIENT
CA One Services, Inc.

DESIGN FIRM
Robert Bailey Incorporated

ALL DESIGN
Dan Franklin

This series of large wall posters combining hand-drawn elements with photography was created using Macromedia FreeHand and Adobe Photoshop on a Power Macintosh 8100.

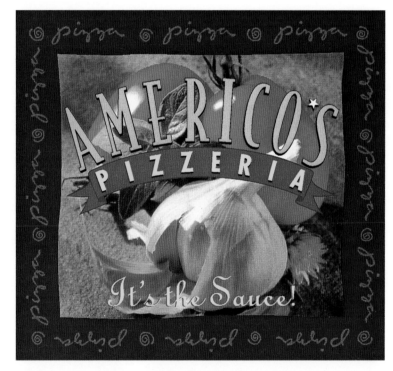

RESTAURANT
Various (Brand identity)

CLIENT
CA One Services, Inc.

DESIGN FIRM
Robert Bailey Incorporated

ALL DESIGN
Dan Franklin

The entire logo, including the type, was drawn by hand and assembled using Adobe Streamline and Macromedia FreeHand on a Power Macintosh.

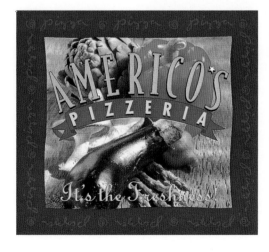

Other Restaurants

RESTAURANT
Geranium Bar

CLIENT
Grand Hotel

DESIGN FIRM
Reeser Advertising & Associates

ART DIRECTOR
Nancy Reeser

DESIGNERS
Nancy Reeser, Debra Zapata

ILLUSTRATORS
Jeff Landis, Mimi Mussen,
Gary Roger, Debra Zapata,
Sherry Vantson

PAPER/PRINTING
100 lb. Astrolite Cover, Classic
Linen Cover, 130 lb. Classic
Linen Avon Brilliant White

Artwork was done in
mechanical form, with color
separations hand-cut
in rubylith. The menu has
five matching pieces.
All prints in three PMS colors,
some with gold foil.

BREAKFAST

JUICES
ORANGE   GRAPEFRUIT
APPLE   CRANBERRY
GRAPE   PASSION FRUIT
TOMATO   VEGETABLE

FRUITS
FRESH BERRIES
HALF GRAPEFRUIT   FRUIT SUPREME
STEWED PRUNES
LOW FAT YOGURT

EGGS
FRIED   SCRAMBLED
POACHED   SHIRRED

OMELETTES
FLORENTINE   SPANISH
HAM and CHEESE   EGGBEATER
SEAFOOD and CREME FRAICHE

CEREALS
OATMEAL with CINNAMON and DRIED FRUIT
DRY CEREALS   GRITS with CORN BREAD

TOAST AND PASTRY BASKET

BREAKFAST ITEMS
BISCUITS with HAM and SAUSAGE GRAVY
PARK AVENUE TOAST, RAISINS and CREAM CHEESE
BLUEBERRY PECAN PANCAKES, Maple Syrup
POACHED FILET OF MACKINAC WHITEFISH, Drawn Butter

HOME FRIED POTATOES   CORN and PEPPER HASH   CANADIAN BACON
RASHER of BACON   SAUSAGE   HONEY CURED HAM

MORNING SPECIALTIES
(at an additional charge of 3.00)

BREAKFAST SIRLOIN STEAK
EGGS BENEDICT
SMOKED SALMON and BAGELS,
with CREAM CHEESE, ONIONS and CAPERS

Always available for our guests:
Margarine, Low-Fat Yogurt, Low-Fat Cottage Cheese, Salt Substitute, Melba Toast

RESTAURANT
Main Dining Room

CLIENT
Grand Hotel

DESIGN FIRM
Reeser Advertising & Associates

ART DIRECTOR
Nancy Reeser

DESIGNERS
Mimi Musser, Nancy Reeser

ILLUSTRATORS
Jeff Landis, Robin Agnew

PAPER/PRINTING
100 lb. Astrolite Cover
Smooth White, 14 pt.
Carolina Cover C2S

The menus have different color borders, allowing the hotel to change the menu every 2 to 3 days, embossed and foiled with a hotel design. Boys' and girls' menus each have their own designs.

RESTAURANT
Celilo

CLIENT
The Governor Hotel

DESIGN FIRM
Jeff Fisher Design

ART DIRECTOR/DESIGNER
Jeff Fisher

The identity for Celilo was pieced together with actual letters from the handwritten journals of Capt. Meriwether Lewis, scanned and used to form necessary words. A cleaner, alternative identity was created by cutting the name from rubylith, which conveyed a handcrafted look.

RESTAURANT/CLIENT
Palena Restaurant

DESIGN FIRM
The Invisions Group Ltd.

ART DIRECTOR
John Cabot Lodge

DESIGNER
Denise Sparhawk

RESTAURANT
Ultimate Burrito

DESIGN FIRM
Jeff Fisher Design

ART DIRECTOR/DESIGNER
Jeff Fisher

This project was created in Macromedia FreeHand.

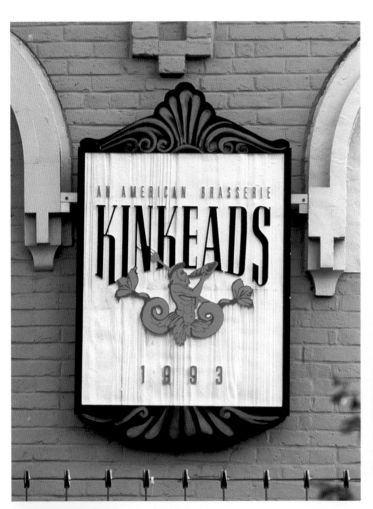

RESTAURANT
Kinkead's

CLIENT
Robert Kinkead

DESIGN FIRM
The Invisions Group Ltd.

ART DIRECTOR
John Cabot Lodge

DESIGNERS
Denise Sparhawk,
Michael Kraine

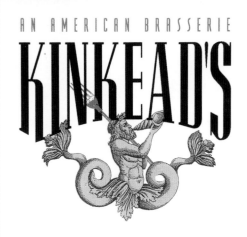

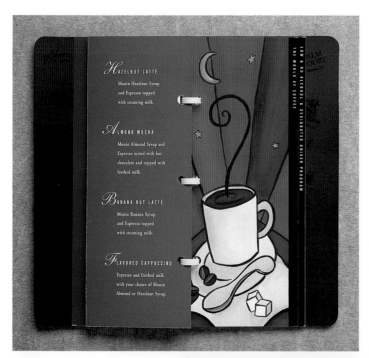

CLIENT
Omni Hotels

DESIGN FIRM
Associates Design

ART DIRECTOR
Chuck Polonsky

DESIGNER/ILLUSTRATOR
Jill Arena

Illustrations were done
in acrylic.

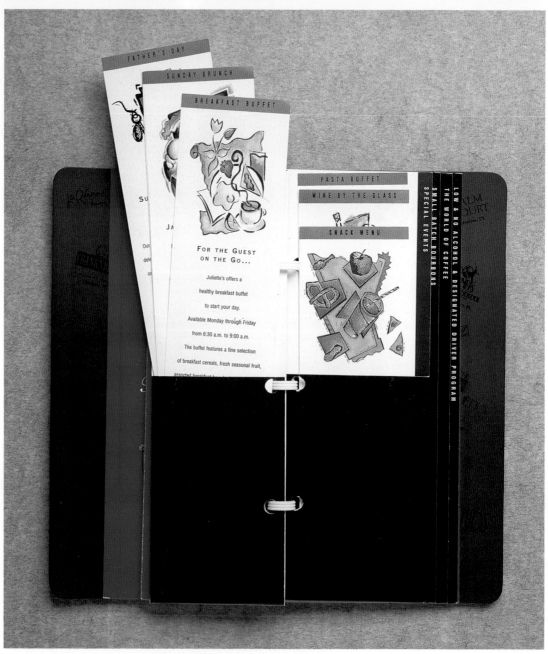

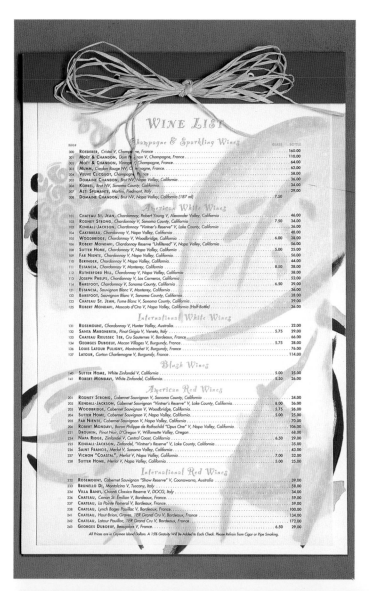

RESTAURANT
Westin Casurian

CLIENT
Columbia Sussex

DESIGN FIRM
Associates Design

ART DIRECTOR
Chuck Polonsky

DESIGNER/ILLUSTRATOR
Mary Greco

RESTAURANT
Prairie Knights Casino

CLIENT
Seven Circles

DESIGN FIRM
Associates Design

ART DIRECTOR
Chuck Polonsky

DESIGNER/ILLUSTRATOR
Jill Arena

PAPER
Wynstone Corrugated Board

CLIENT
Hyatt Hotels

DESIGN FIRM
Associates Design

ART DIRECTOR
Chuck Polonsky

DESIGNER
Jill Arena

PHOTOGRAPHER
Scott Simms

PAPER
Carolina Cover

MAMA LOO'S

RESTAURANT
Mama Loo's

CLIENT
Atlantis Resort

DESIGN FIRM
Associates Design

ART DIRECTOR
Chuck Polonsky

DESIGNER/ILLUSTRATOR
Mary Greco

CLIENT
The Millenium Hilton

DESIGN FIRM
Associates Design

ART DIRECTOR
Chuck Polonsky

DESIGNER/ILLUSTRATOR
Beth Finn

CLIENT
Omni Hotels

DESIGN FIRM
Associates Design

ART DIRECTOR
Chuck Polonsky

DESIGNER
Jill Arena

ILLUSTRATOR
Beth Finn

PAPER
Carolina

The illustration was created
with marker and colored pencil.

CLIENT
Hotel Sofitel Minneapolis

DESIGN FIRM
Associates Design

ART DIRECTOR
Chuck Polonsky

DESIGNER
Jill Arena

PAPER
Splendorlux

This was a wedding menu.

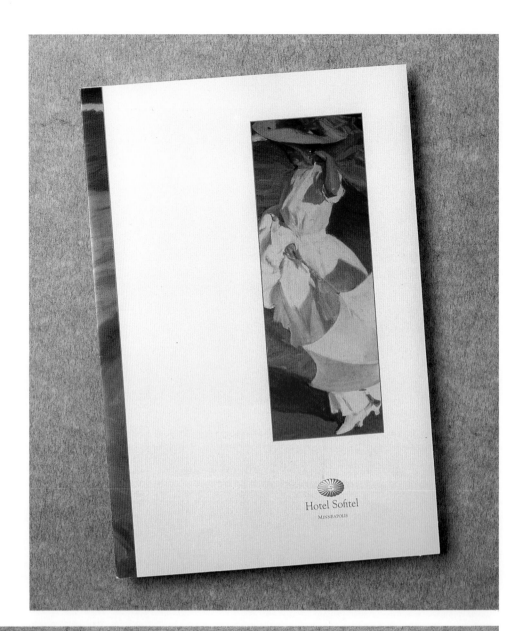

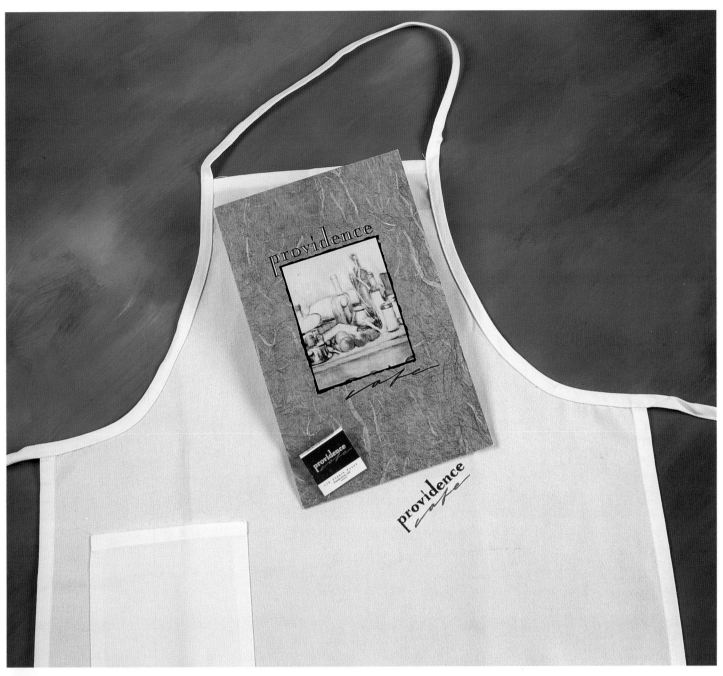

RESTAURANT
Providence Cafe

CLIENT
Harding Stone

DESIGN FIRM
Sean Murphy Associates, Ltd.

ART DIRECTOR
Sean Murphy

DESIGNERS
Sean Murphy, Christine Faut

PAPER/PRINTING
Mac Papers

Handmade paper was used
for the outside background.
Sean Murphy developed
a brushstroke background
for the inside.

RESTAURANT
95 School Street

CLIENT
School Street Corp.

DESIGNER/ILLUSTRATOR
Barbara Maslen

PAPER/PRINTING
Speckletone Text,
Xerox Color Copy

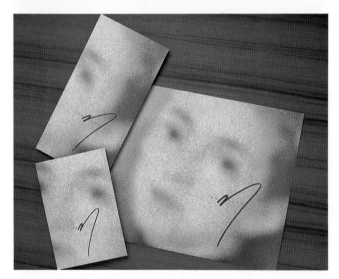

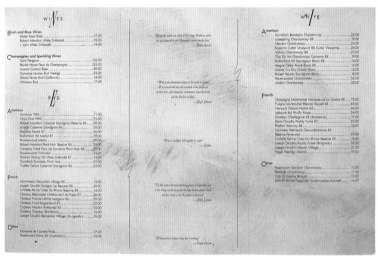

RESTAURANT
Jonnick's

DESIGN FIRM
Sean Murphy Associates, Ltd.

ART DIRECTOR/DESIGNER
Sean Murphy

PHOTOGRAPHER
David Bell

Background texture outside of
menu is a Renoir painting
close-up and out of focus.

RESTAURANT
Jeffrey's

CLIENT
Jeff Jennings/Jeffrey's

DESIGN FIRM
Sean Murphy Associates, Ltd.

DESIGNERS
Mary Lawing (menu),
Christine Faut (logo)

This project was done
in Macromedia FreeHand.

RESTAURANT/CLIENT
Pizza Picasso

DESIGN FIRM
Bullet Communications Inc.

ALL DESIGN
Tim Scott

Hand-drawn type
and illustration.

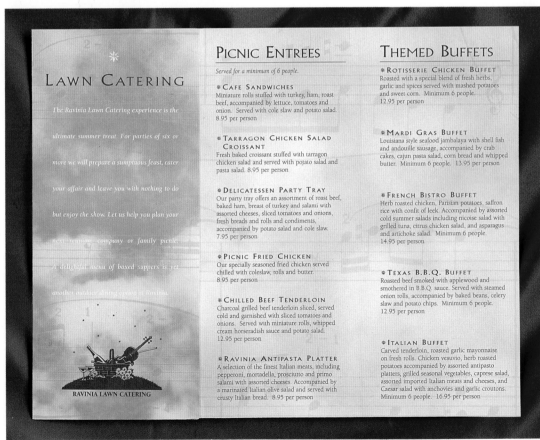

LAWN CATERING

The Ravinia Lawn Catering experience is the

ultimate summer treat. For parties of six or

more we will prepare a sumptuous feast, cater

your affair and leave you with nothing to do

but enjoy the show. Let us help you plan your

next evening company or family picnic.

A delightful menu of boxed suppers is yet

another outdoor dining option at Ravinia.

RAVINIA LAWN CATERING

PICNIC ENTREES

Served for a minimum of 6 people.

✳ CAFE SANDWICHES
Miniature rolls stuffed with turkey, ham, roast
beef, accompanied by lettuce, tomatoes and
onion. Served with cole slaw and potato salad.
8.95 per person

**✳ TARRAGON CHICKEN SALAD
CROISSANT**
Fresh baked croissant stuffed with tarragon
chicken salad and served with potato salad and
pasta salad. 8.95 per person

✳ DELICATESSEN PARTY TRAY
Our party tray offers an assortment of roast beef,
baked ham, breast of turkey and salami with
assorted cheeses, sliced tomatoes and onions,
fresh breads and rolls and condiments,
accompanied by potato salad and cole slaw.
7.95 per person

✳ PICNIC FRIED CHICKEN
Our specially seasoned fried chicken served
chilled with coleslaw, rolls and butter.
8.95 per person

✳ CHILLED BEEF TENDERLOIN
Charcoal grilled beef tenderloin sliced, served
cold and garnished with sliced tomatoes and
onions. Served with miniature rolls, whipped
cream horseradish sauce and potato salad.
12.95 per person

✳ RAVINIA ANTIPASTA PLATTER
A selection of the finest Italian meats, including
pepperoni, mortadella, prosciutto and primo
salami with assorted cheeses. Accompanied by
a marinated Italian olive salad and served with
crusty Italian bread. 8.95 per person

THEMED BUFFETS

✳ ROTISSERIE CHICKEN BUFFET
Roasted with a special blend of fresh herbs,
garlic and spices served with mashed potatoes
and sweet corn. Minimum 6 people.
12.95 per person.

✳ MARDI GRAS BUFFET
Louisiana style seafood jambalaya with shell fish
and andouille sausage, accompanied by crab
cakes, cajun pasta salad, corn bread and whipped
butter. Minimum 6 people. 13.95 per person

✳ FRENCH BISTRO BUFFET
Herb roasted chicken, Parisian potatoes, saffron
rice with confit of leek. Accompanied by assorted
cold summer salads including nicoise salad with
grilled tuna, citrus chicken salad, and asparagus
and artichoke salad. Minimum 6 people.
14.95 per person

✳ TEXAS B.B.Q. BUFFET
Roasted beef smoked with applewood and
smothered in B.B.Q. sauce. Served with steamed
onion rolls, accompanied by baked beans, celery
slaw and potato chips. Minimum 6 people.
12.95 per person

✳ ITALIAN BUFFET
Carved tenderloin, roasted garlic mayonnaise
on fresh rolls. Chicken vesuvio, herb roasted
potatoes accompanied by assorted antipasto
platters, grilled seasonal vegetables, caprese salad,
assorted imported Italian meats and cheeses, and
Caesar salad with anchovies and garlic croutons.
Minimum 6 people. 16.95 per person

RESTAURANT
Ravinia Lawn Catering Menu

CLIENT
Ravinia

DESIGN FIRM
The Levy Restaurants

CREATIVE DIRECTOR
Marcy L. Young

ILLUSTRATOR
Claire Baldwin

RESTAURANT
Passerelle

DESIGN FIRM
Shamlian Advertising

ART DIRECTOR
Fred Shamlian

DESIGNER
Stephen Bagi

ILLUSTRATORS
Heidi Stevens, Susan Harvey,
Ginger DiMaio

PHOTOGRAPHERS
Barry Halkin, Joe Farley

PAPER/PRINTING
Kimdura paper, Graphicolor

A black-and-white photo was
scanned into Adobe Photoshop,
enhanced in various ways,
then output for retouching and
hand-coloring. The color
version was re-scanned, and
several Photoshop and plug-in
effects were used to create
a grainy, pastel texture.

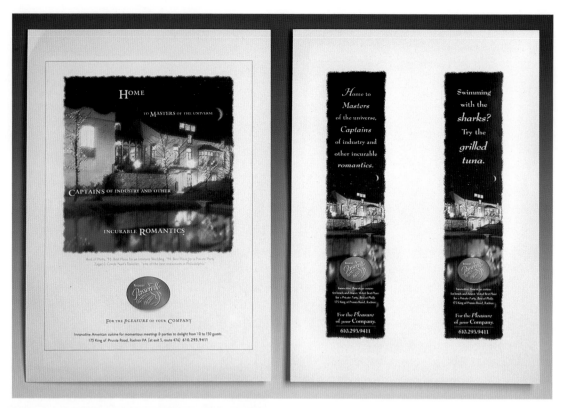

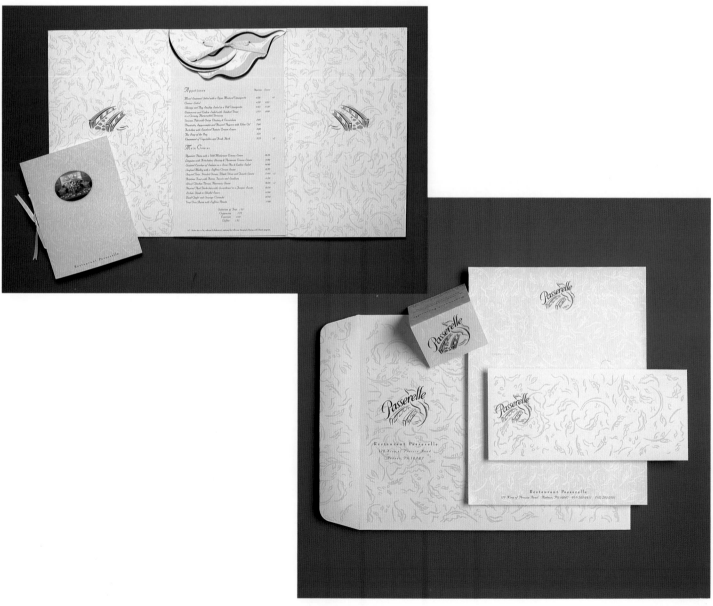

GRAT!S

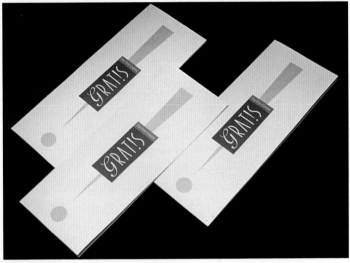

RESTAURANT/CLIENT
Gratis Restaurant

DESIGN FIRM
Bright & Associates

ART DIRECTORS
Bill Corridori, Keith Bright

DESIGNER/ILLUSTRATOR
Bill Corridori

Designed and illustrated
in Adobe Illustrator
with a custom typeface.

RESTAURANT
Bailey's

DESIGN FIRM
Mind's Eye Studio

ART DIRECTOR/DESIGNER
Valery Mercer

ILLUSTRATOR
Michael Downs

PAPER/PRINTING
Kraft Paper,
metallic and black inks

All the illustrations were hand-
drawn, in black and white
then broken down into color,
produced on a Macintosh
with QuarkXPress.

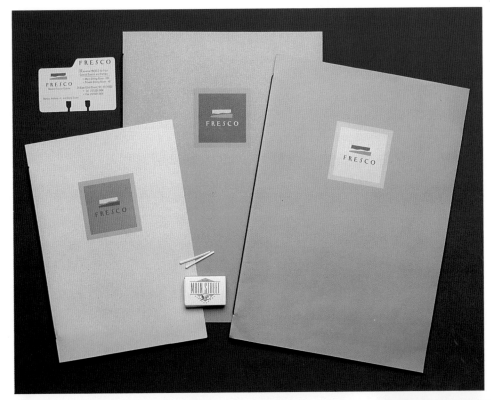

RESTAURANT
Fresco

CLIENT
Marion Scotto

DESIGN FIRM
PM Design

ART DIRECTOR/DESIGNER
Philip Marzo

PHOTOGRAPHER
Geoff Reed

RESTAURANT
Anzu

DESIGN FIRM
David Carter Design

ALL DESIGN
Sharon LeJeune

PAPER
Imported handmade and
Simpson Quest

A typographic "chop" was
created and hand-stamped
on the handmade paper.
The insert pages were
produced in QuarkXPress and
laser printed on earth-toned
paper, then assembled by hand
with
a vine and leather binding.

RESTAURANT/CLIENT
The Marsh Restaurant

DESIGN FIRM
Design Center

ART DIRECTOR
John Reger

DESIGNER
Kobe

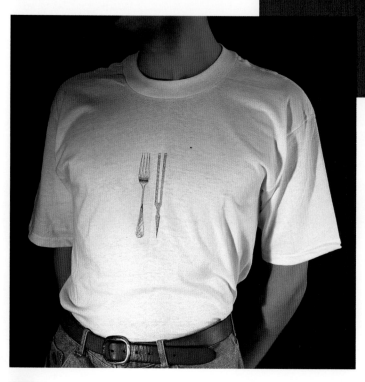

GREENE STREET

RESTAURANT
Green Street

CLIENT
Tony Goldman

DESIGN FIRM
Sagmeister Inc.

ART DIRECTOR/DESIGNER
Stefan Sagmeister

RESTAURANT/CLIENT
Harvest Restaurant

DESIGN FIRM
Clifford Selbert Design

ART DIRECTOR/DESIGNER
Melanie Lowe

ILLUSTRATORS
Mark Fisher, Melanie Lowe

PHOTOGRAPHER
Susie Cushner

PAPER/PRINTING
Champion Chromecote
Recycled, offset

Different photos or illustrations
were used to personalize
each area of the restaurant.

RESTAURANT
Essex Street Bagel Exchange

DESIGN FIRM
Cornerstone

ART DIRECTOR
Keith Steimel

DESIGNER
Paul McDowall

All work for this project
was assembled in
Macromedia FreeHand.

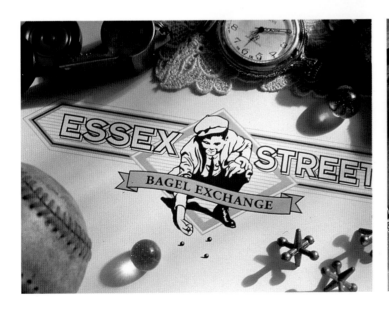

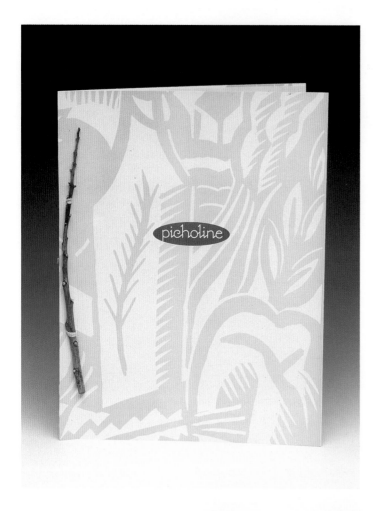

RESTAURANT
Picholine

DESIGN FIRM
Louise Fili Ltd.

ART DIRECTOR/DESIGNER
Louise Fili

ILLUSTRATOR
Anthony Russo

This menu was bound with a rosemary branch, allowing for changing pages frequently.

RESTAURANT
Pleiades

DESIGN FIRM
Louise Fili Ltd.

ART DIRECTOR/DESIGNER
Louise Fili

ILLUSTRATOR
Anthony Russo

PAPER/PRINTING
Laser-print on vellum

RESTAURANT
Oak Grill

CLIENT
Ojai Valley Inn

DESIGN FIRM
HBA International / Graphis

ALL DESIGN
Kevin Scholberg

RESTAURANT
Hawthorne Lane

CLIENT
Hawthorne Lane Partners

DESIGN FIRM
Hunt Weber Clark Associates

ART DIRECTOR
Nancy Hunt-Weber

DESIGNER
Gary Williams

ILLUSTRATORS
Nancy Hunt-Weber,
Gary Williams

PAPER/PRINTING
Speckletone, Cordtone

RESTAURANT
Chelsea Restaurant and Bar

CLIENT
Westin Chicago

DESIGN FIRM
Sayles Graphic Design

ALL DESIGN
John Sayles

PHOTOGRAPHER
Bill Nellans

PAPER/PRINTING
Graphika! Antique parchment

The burgundy, navy and tan menu covers were printed in complementary inks, with gold tassel closures to hold the menu inside.

RESTAURANT
Capital Club

DESIGN FIRM
Sayles Graphic Design

ALL DESIGN
John Sayles

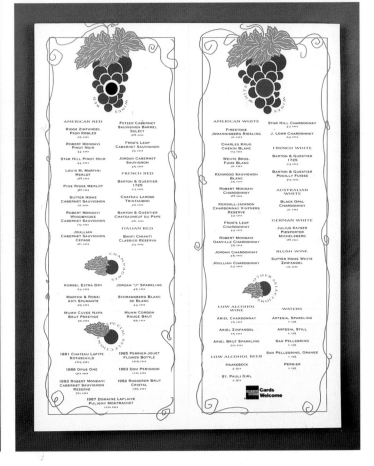

RESTAURANT
Eagle's Nest

DESIGN FIRM
Val Gene Associates

ART DIRECTOR/DESIGNER
Lacy Leverett

PRODUCTION
Shirley Morrow

PHOTOGRAPHER
Chuck Doswell III

Directory

ADRIENNE WEISS CORPORATION
c/o The Levy Restaurants
980 North Michigan Avenue
Suite 400
Chicago, IL 60611

ADVENTURE ADVERTISING
P. O. Box 576
Camden, ME 04843

ARTIE HOROWITZ DESIGN
632 South Highland Avenue
Los Angeles, CA 90036

ASSOCIATES DESIGN
3177 MacArthur Boulevard
Northbrook, IL 60062

AWG GRAPHICS BUREAU E CONSULT. INF. LTDA.
R. Maestro Cardim 377 G84
Bela Vista, Sao Paulo SP
Brazil

THE BEAIRD AGENCY
2828 Routh Street
Suite 750
Dallas, TX 75081

BETTY SOLDI
29 Sheen Common Drive
Richmond. Surrey
TW10 5BW
England

BRIGHT & ASSOCIATES
901 Abbotkinney
Venice, CA 90291

BRILLBANK CREATIVE CONSULTANTS SDN. BHD.
5, Jalan Timur
46000 Retaling Jaya, Selangov
Malaysia

BULLET COMMUNICATIONS INC.
200 South Midland Avenue
Joliet, IL 60435

CLIFFORD SELBERT DESIGN
2067 Massachusetts Avenue
Cambridge, MA 02140

CORE GRAPHICS
2033A Giribaldi Way
Whistler, British Colombia
Canada VON 1B2

CORNERSTONE
444 Park Avenue South
New York, NY 10016

DAVID CARTER DESIGN
4112 Swiss Avenue
Dallas, TX 75204

DEAN JOHNSON DESIGN
604 Fort Wayne Avenue
Indianapolis, IN 46204

DESIGN CENTER
15119 Minnetonka Boulevard
Minnetonka, MN 55345

HECTOR DI LUZIO
Terrero 2981 OF.3
San Isidro
Argentina

DISNEY DESIGN GROUP
Walt Disney World
P. O. Box 10,000
Lake Buena Vista, FL 32830-1000

ENTERPRISE FOUR
15 Signal Road
Stamford, CT 06902

FACTORY WERBEAGENTUR
Reichenbachstrasse 33
D-80469 Munich
Germany

GAF ADVERTISING/DESIGN
4115 Rawlins Street
Dallas, TX 75219-3661

GLEN GROUP MARKETING AND ADVERTISING
Tin Mine Road
P. O. Box 524
Jackson, NH 03846

GRETEMAN GROUP
142 North Mosley
Wichita, KS 67202

HANSON ASSOCIATES, INC.
133 Grape Street
Philadelphia, PA 19127

HARRIS & LOVE, INC.
630 East South Temple
Salt Lake City, UT 84102

HBA INTERNATIONAL/GRAPHIS
909 West Peachtree Street NE
Atlanta, GA 30309

HEATHER HEFLIN
CAA Box 801
Bloomfield Hills, MI 48303

HORNALL ANDERSON DESIGN WORKS, INC.
1008 Western Avenue
Suite 600
Seattle, WA 98104

HUNT WEBER CLARK ASSOCIATES
525 Brannan Street
Suite #302
San Francisco, CA 94107

I.D. ZIGN CO.
329 Box Elder Drive
West Chester, PA 19380

THE INVISIONS GROUP LTD.
4927 Auburn Avenue
Suite 100
Bethesda, MD 20814-2641

JEFF FISHER DESIGN
P. O. Box 6631
Portland, OR 97228

JOHN EVANS DESIGN
2200 North Lamar #220
Dallas, TX 75023

TIMMY KAN
524 Pak Suet House
Choi Hung Estate
Kowloon, Hong Kong

KAPP & ASSOCIATES, INC.
2729 Prospect Avenue
Cleveland, OH 44115

LANCE ANDERSON DESIGN
22 Margrave Place
Studio 5
San Francisco, CA 94133

LAURA JACOBY
501 South 16th Street, 4R
Philadelphia, PA 19146

THE LEVY RESTAURANTS
980 North Michigan Avenue
Suite 400
Chicago, IL 60611

LOUISE FILI LTD.
71 5th Avenue
New York, NY 10003

EMMA MAIN
P. O. Box 11-331 Wellington
Harcourts Building, Suite 316
22 Grey Street
New Zealand

MALLEN AND FRIENDS
8522 Cherokee Lane
Leawood, KS 66206

MARVE COOPER DESIGN, LTD.
2120 West Grand
Chicago, IL 60612

BARBARA MASLEN
55 Bayview Avenue
Sag Harbor, NY 11963

MCELVENEY & PALOZZI GRAPHIC DESIGN GROUP
1255 University Avenue
Rochester, NY 14607

MEHUL DESIGN
2408 East Johnson Road
Atlanta, GA 30345

THE MENU WORKSHOP
2200 6th Avenue
Suite 400
Seattle, WA 98121

MIND'S EYE STUDIO
P. O. Box 194
East Kelowna
British Columbia V0H 1G0
Canada

PAGE DESIGN, INC.
1900 29th Street
Sacramento, CA 95816

PANDAMONIUM DESIGNS
14 Mount Hood Road
Suite J
Boston, MA 02146

GLORIA PAUL
150 West Jefferson Avenue
Suite 100
Detroit, MI 48226

PENTAGRAM DESIGN
204 Fifth Avenue
New York, NY 10010

PLANET DESIGN COMPANY
605 Williamson Street
Madison, WI 53703

PM DESIGN
11 Maple Terrace
Verona, NJ 07044

PPA DESIGN LIMITED
11 Macdonnell Road D-3
Midlevels, Hong Kong

RAINWATER DESIGN
63 Congress Street
Hartford, CT 06114

RAVEN MADD DESIGN COMPANY
P. O. Box 11331 Wellington
Level 3 Harcourts Building
Corner Grey Street and Lambton Quay
New Zealand

REESER ADVERTISING & ASSOCIATES
1325 Snell Isle Boulevard NE #219
St. Petersburg, FL 33704

ROBERT BAILEY INCORPORATED
0121 SW Bancroft Street
Portland, OR 97201

RUSSEK ADVERTISING
1500 Broadway
24th Floor
New York, NY 10036

RUSSELL LEONG DESIGN
847 Emerson Street
Palo Alto, CA 94301

RUSTY KAY & ASSOCIATES
2665 Main Street
Suite F
Santa Monica, CA 90405

SAGMEISTER INC.
222 West 14th Street
New York, NY 10011

SAYLES GRAPHIC DESIGN
308 Eighth Street
Des Moines, IA 50309

SCOTT WRIGHT DESIGN
1 Northbrook Drive #106
Manchester, NH 03102

SEAN MURPHY ASSOCIATES, LTD.
505-H South Cedar Street
Charlotte, NC 28202

SHAMLIAN ADVERTISING
128 Mansion Drive
Media, PA 19063

SHELLEY DANYSH STUDIO
8940 Krewstown Road #107
Philadelphia, PA 19115

TOM FOWLER, INC.
9 Webbs Hill Road
Stamford, CT 06903

TONY MURCIA DESIGN
901 West Neely Avenue
Muncie, IN 47303

VAL GENE ASSOCIATES
5208 Classen Boulevard
Oklahoma City, OK 73118

VRONTIKIS DESIGN OFFICE
2021 Pontius Avenue
Los Angeles, CA 90025

WHITNEY-EDWARDS DESIGN
14 West Dover Street
P. O. Box 2425
Easton, MD 21601

WICKY'S GRAPHICS
7102 Wayne Avenue
Upper Darby, PA 19082-3614

WTS STUDIOS
401 Fountainhead Circle #250
Kissimmee, FL 34741

ZANDE NEWMAN DESIGN
2727 Prytania, No. 5
New Orleans, LA 701??

Index